Naval Operations Concept

2010

*Implementing
The Maritime Strategy*

The basic premise of our newly published Maritime Strategy is that the United States is a force for good in the world—that while we are capable of launching a clenched fist when we must—offering the hand of friendship is also an essential and prominent tool in our kit. That premise flows from the belief that preventing wars means we don't have to win wars.

 — General James T. Conway, USMC

We do more than just respond; we prevent. In our Maritime Strategy we state that we believe that it is just as important to prevent wars as it is to win wars. That is done through our worldwide presence, our well-trained Sailors, and our very capable ships, airplanes, and submarines.

 — Admiral Gary Roughead, USN

The Coast Guard completely subscribes to this strategy. It reinforces the Coast Guard Strategy for Safety, Security, and Stewardship and it reflects not only the global reach of our maritime services, but the need to integrate, synchronize and act with coalition and international partners to not only win wars—but to prevent wars.

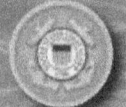 — Admiral Thad W. Allen, USCG

Preface

The daily service and sacrifice of Sailors, Marines, and Coast Guardsmen are constant reminders that we are a Nation at war. As we continue to stabilize Iraq and counter a resurgent Taliban in Afghanistan, extremist ideologues, terrorists, criminals and rogue states still mar the international landscape, promoting their interests by undermining global stability. Concurrently, several key regional powers continue to significantly enhance their own military capabilities. To deal with the expanding range of these challenges, we must always be prepared and ready to assume new missions—today and tomorrow.

Four years ago the Navy and Marine Corps presented a unified vision for the future—*Naval Operations Concept 2006* (NOC 06). It served as an intellectual stimulus for evolving our Maritime Strategy to meet the challenges of the 21st century. The Navy and Marine Corps, joined by our seagoing partner, the U.S. Coast Guard, explored the ideas articulated in NOC 06 to inform development of our new Maritime Strategy. With the publication of *A Cooperative Strategy for 21ˢᵗ Century Seapower* (CS-21) in October 2007, NOC 06 fulfilled its purpose.

Naval Operations Concept 2010 (NOC 10) describes when, where and how U.S. naval forces will contribute to enhancing security, preventing conflict and prevailing in war. NOC 10 is not designed for a cursory reading; it is a publication intended for serious study by professionals. Readers will quickly discern several themes that collectively embody the essence of naval service to our Nation. Implicit in these themes is that Sailors, Marines, and Coast Guardsmen should expect to be engaged in both preventing and winning wars. These themes reflect the content of CS-21 as well as the guidance provided by the Secretary of Defense in the *National Defense Strategy* (NDS) and the 2010 Quadrennial Defense Review (QDR).

The sea services have a long history of accomplishing diverse missions, from protecting American merchantmen during an undeclared naval war in the late 18th century, to establishing our naval prowess in the War of 1812, to suppressing the African slave trade and West Indian piracy in the 19th century, to fighting the major wars and confronting the irregular challenges of the 20th century. As the 21st century unfolds, we must continue to be effective warriors as well as informed and articulate ambassadors, serving our Nation's interests and facilitating free global interaction from the sea.

James T. Conway

General, U.S. Marine Corps
Commandant of the Marine Corps

Gary Roughead

Admiral, U.S. Navy
Chief of Naval Operations

Thad W. Allen

Admiral, U.S. Coast Guard
Commandant of the Coast Guard

The pathway of man's journey through the ages is littered with the wreckage of nations, which, in their hour of glory, forgot their dependence on the seas.

—Brigadier General James D. Hittle, USMC (Retired), 1961 Military Historian and Theorist

Contents

Nor must Uncle Sam's web-feet be forgotten.
At all the watery margins they have been present.
Not only in the deep sea, the broad bay, and
the rapid river, but also up the narrow muddy bayou,
and wherever the ground was a little damp,
they have been and made their tracks.

—President Abraham Lincoln, 1863
16th President of the United States

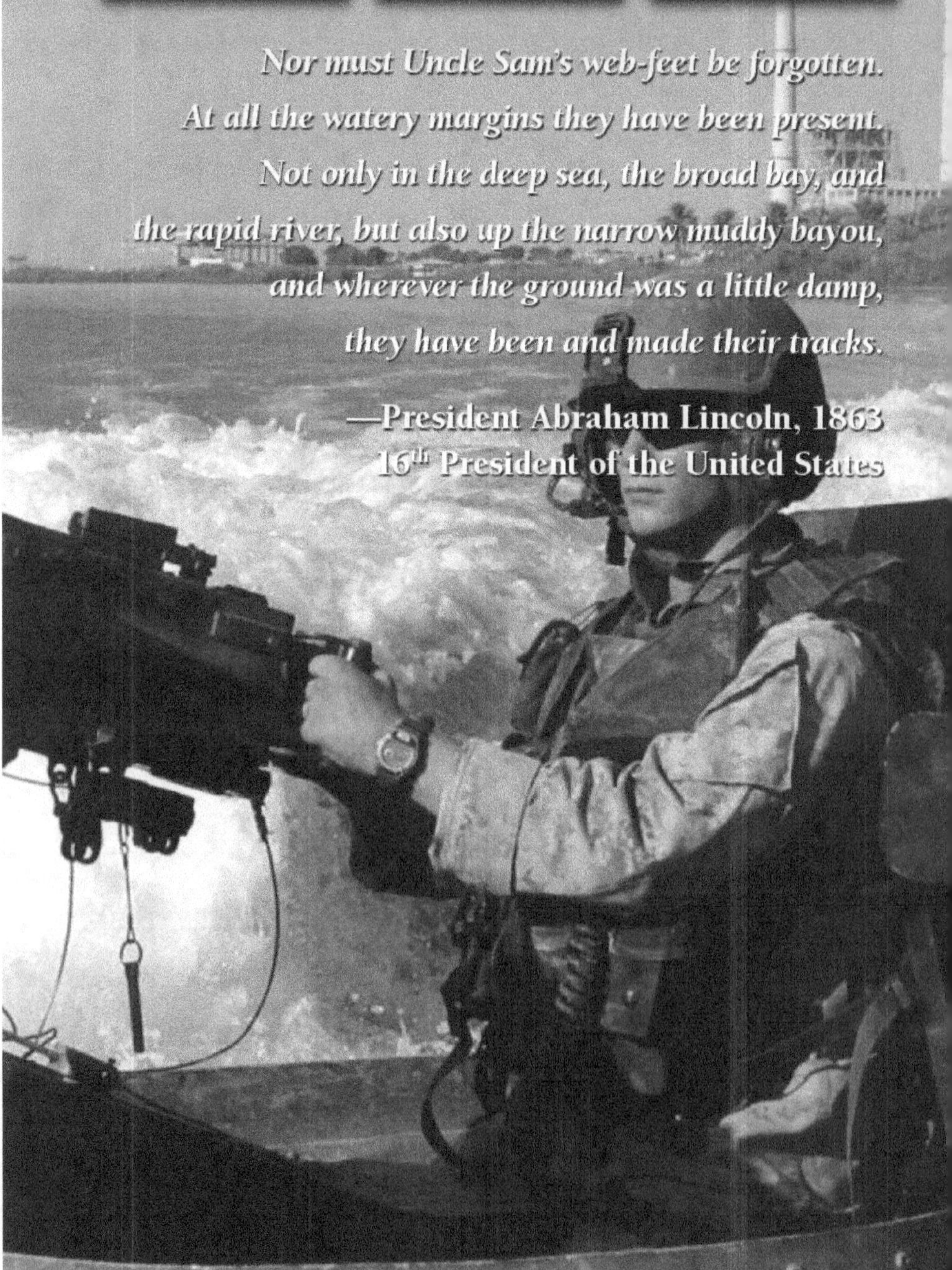

Chapter 1
Introduction

As we think about this range of threats, it is common to define and divide the so-called "high end" from the "low end," the conventional from the irregular; armored divisions on one side, guerrillas toting AK-47s on the other. In reality...the categories of warfare are blurring and do not fit into neat, tidy boxes. We can expect to see more tools and tactics of destruction— from the sophisticated to the simple—being employed simultaneously in hybrid and more complex forms of warfare.

—Robert M. Gates, 22nd Secretary of Defense,
29 September 2008

Purpose

Naval Operations Concept 2010 (NOC 10) describes when, where and how U.S. naval forces will contribute to enhancing security, preventing conflict and prevailing in war in order to guide Maritime Strategy implementation in a manner consistent with national strategy. NOC 10 describes the *ways* with which the sea services will achieve the *ends* articulated in *A Cooperative Strategy for 21ˢᵗ Century Seapower* (CS-21).

Relationship to Other Documents

NOC 10 supersedes NOC 06 and represents the evolution in naval operational concepts and capabilities needed to adapt to the relentless efforts of current and potential adversaries to find advantage in the maritime domain. Continuous innovation, by the United States, its allies and partners, and its adversaries, compels NOC 10 to be a contemporary document that guides current operations, as well as a forward looking effort to anticipate and describe the ways new capabilities can be integrated into joint force efforts to address emerging threats. In this regard, NOC 10 articulates how naval capabilities can be applied in support of the combatant commanders' operations, contingency plans, and theater security cooperation (TSC) plans.

Scope

The integration of naval capabilities to achieve specific joint mission objectives is the responsibility of commanders, who formulate their concepts of operations to achieve advantage and decision. In contrast, Service operational concepts are designed to describe the capabilities that operational commanders can expect the Services to provide, and indicate selected ways these capabilities can be integrated to achieve mission success. Consequently, NOC 10 is designed to inform development of joint concepts, plans and experimentation. The term "naval" and "the Naval Service" are used throughout this publication to encompass Navy, Marine Corps, and Coast Guard personnel and organizations.[1]

NOC 10 articulates the ways naval forces are employed to achieve the strategy conveyed in CS-21. Published in 2007, CS-21 described a set of core capabilities that added maritime security and humanitarian assistance and disaster response (HA/DR) to the traditional forward presence, deterrence, sea control, and power projection. Not to be viewed as discrete missions or functions, these core capabilities are intrinsically linked and mutually supporting enablers for achieving the Naval Service's strategic imperatives:

Regionally concentrated, credible combat power to:
- Limit regional conflict with deployed, decisive maritime power
- Deter major power war
- Win our Nation's wars

Globally distributed, mission-tailored maritime forces to:
- Contribute to homeland defense in depth
- Foster and sustain cooperative relationships with more international partners
- Prevent or contain local disruptions before they impact the global system

NOC 10 does not prescribe Naval Service *tactics*, nor is it *doctrine*. Rather, it serves as a *precursor to the development of both*. It describes how the Navy, Marine Corps, and Coast Guard operate together, and will be complemented by Service-specific concepts. Collectively, the ideas put forth are to be applied, tested, analyzed and refined through war games, exercises, experiments, and operational lessons learned. This innovation will ultimately inform future revisions of the NOC, as it is updated to remain relevant in the evolving security environment.

In an increasingly complex world, naval forces provide the Nation with the global presence and the freedom of maneuver needed to influence world events. Persistently postured forward, naval forces are continuously engaged with global partners in cooperative security activities aimed at reducing instability and providing another arm of national diplomacy. Their expeditionary capabilities enable and support the joint force effort to combat both conventional and irregular challenges. NOC 10 describes how naval forces will blend "soft" and "hard" power[2] in support of the approach, objectives and enduring national interests articulated in the National Defense Strategy (NDS). These enduring interests include "protecting the nation and our allies from attack or coercion, promoting international security to reduce conflict and foster economic growth, and securing the global commons and with them access to world markets and resources."[3] NOC 10 also expounds upon CS-21's core capabilities: forward presence, maritime security, HA/DR, sea control, power projection and deterrence.

The organization of NOC 10 is not meant to imply, and does not reflect the relative importance of the Naval Service's core capabilities. NOC 10 is presented in a sequence designed to describe how globally dispersed naval forces conducting an array of steady state activities designed to prevent war will, when required, come together to prevail in crisis response or combat operations. NOC 10 describes *The Naval Service* in Chapter 2, followed by *The Overarching Concept: The Sea as Maneuver Space* in Chapter 3. Each of the six subsequent chapters is dedicated to one of the core capabilities. Chapter 4 describes how *Forward Presence* enables the Naval Service to build partner capacity while facilitating its ability to perform all other missions. Chapter 5, *Maritime Security*, describes how naval forces will partner with others to promote safety, economic security, and homeland defense in depth. Similarly, Chapter 6 describes how naval forces will contribute to *HA/DR*. Chapters 7 and 8, *Sea Control* and *Power Projection*, describe how naval forces fulfill their warfighting responsibilities as part of a joint or combined force. Chapter 9 describes how the activities articulated in the preceding five chapters contribute to expanded *Deterrence*. Finally, Chapter 10 will discuss the *Future Force Structure* that supports the implementation of this concept on a global basis.

Annex A describes the relationship between NOC 10 and joint concept development and experimentation. Annex B provides a glossary and endnotes. Unless otherwise noted, all definitions included in this publication are drawn from Joint Publication 1-02, the *Department of Defense Dictionary of Military and Associated Terms.*

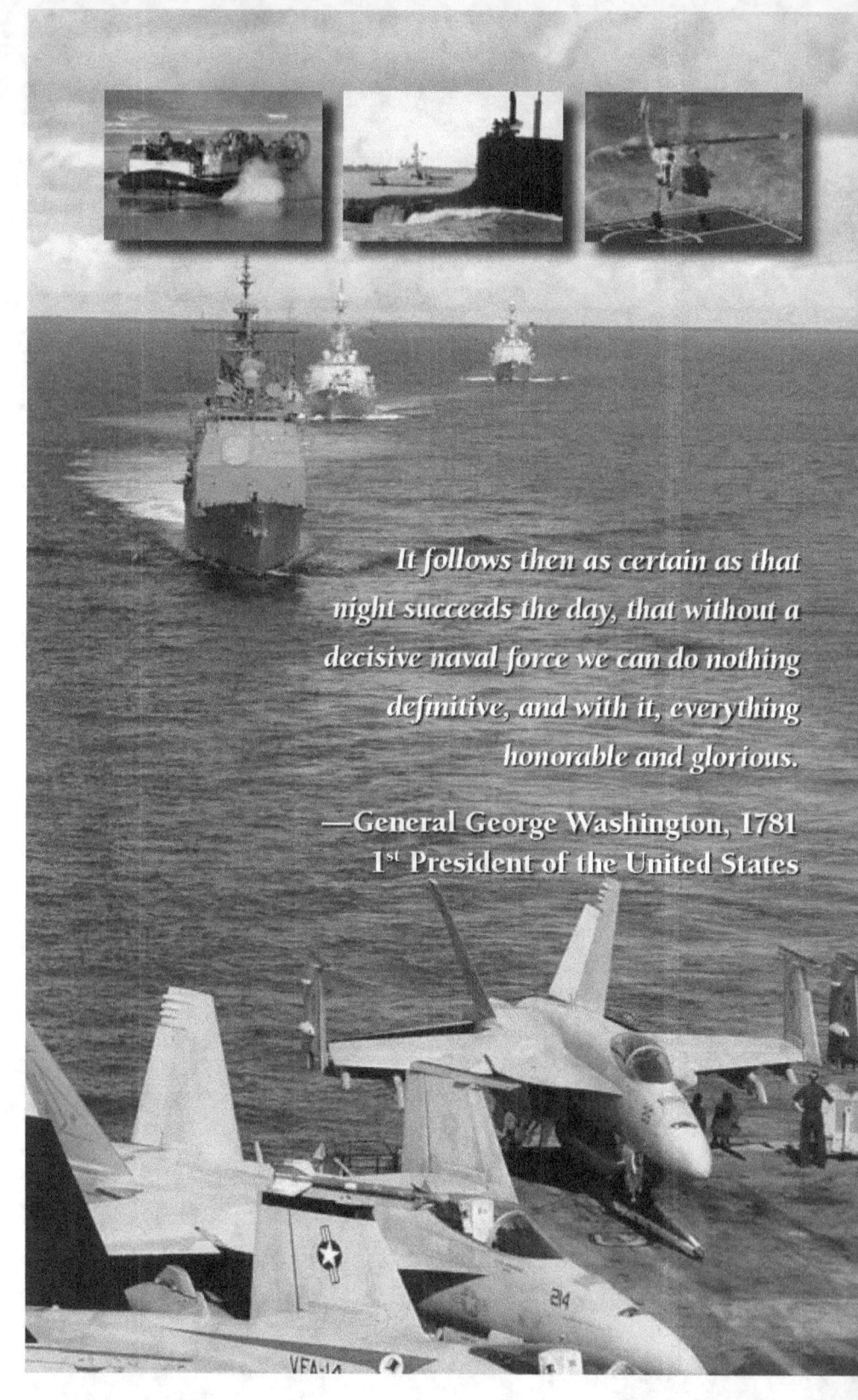

It follows then as certain as that night succeeds the day, that without a decisive naval force we can do nothing definitive, and with it, everything honorable and glorious.

—General George Washington, 1781
1st President of the United States

Chapter 2
The Naval Service

We will always be prepared, so we may always be free.

—President Ronald Reagan, 1984
40th President of the United States

Who We Are

The Naval Service is comprised of the active and reserve components and the civilian personnel of the United States Navy, the United States Marine Corps and the United States Coast Guard.

We are, first and foremost, men and women dedicated to the service of our Nation in peace and war. We are an all-volunteer force instilled with a warrior and guardian ethos. Our people are the foundation of our mission success. They possess willpower, creativity, inspiration, reason, knowledge, and experience to overcome adversity and accomplish any task. They exemplify the values of honor, courage, and commitment.

We are an instrument of national power, employed to prevent conflict and, if necessary, prevail in war. We are organized, trained, and equipped primarily to operate and fight at and from the sea. The qualities that allow us to prevail in war also contribute to conflict prevention. These qualities include *speed, flexibility, agility, scalability, readiness, mobility, self-sustainability,* and *lethality.*

What We Believe

We believe that the future is uncertain, and that the United States will be threatened by a variety of state and non-state adversaries, current and emerging. We believe that both state and non-state adversaries are likely to employ a hybrid of conventional and irregular methods to counter the United States' advantage in conventional military operations. Thus, we must be prepared to overcome a range of adversaries employing a variety of capabilities and tactics.

We believe that naval forces uniquely contribute to overcoming diplomatic, military, and geographic impediments to access, while respecting the sovereignty of nations. Even as security, stability, and the global economy become more interdependent, resistance to a large U.S. military "footprint" abroad will continue to increase. Naval forces provide the ideal means in such a security environment to accomplish a wide variety of missions conducted independently or in concert with joint, interagency, international and non-governmental partners that share the United States' interest in promoting a safe and prosperous world.

We believe that preventing war is as important as winning, and that prevention activities will constitute the most likely application of naval power.

Where We Operate

The Naval Service operates in the *maritime domain*, which consists of the "oceans, seas, bays, estuaries, islands, coastal areas, and the airspace above these, including the littorals." The *littoral* is comprised of two segments. The *seaward* portion is that area from the open ocean to the shore that must be controlled to support operations ashore. The *landward* portion is the area inland from the shore that can be supported and defended directly from the sea.

A number of common, non-doctrinal terms also describe aspects of the maritime domain. *Blue water* refers to the open ocean; *green water* refers to coastal waters, ports and harbors; and *brown water* refers to navigable rivers and their estuaries.

The complexity of the maritime domain, which encompasses the confluence of water, air, land, as well as space and cyberspace, is infinite in its variations. As a result, operations in the maritime domain are inherently challenging. The magnitude of this challenge increases as the proximity to land increases, with the most complex cases being operations that transition between water and land.

This is the environment in which naval forces thrive.

Naval forces will continue to be in high demand across the range of military operations (ROMO)[4], largely because they effectively bridge the seams between water, land, and air. Leveraging our strong historic interdependencies, we task organize Navy, Marine Corps, and Coast Guard resources to achieve the requisite blend of capability, capacity, and legal authorities to suit the given situation and mission. Similarly, command relationships are tailored to each operation based on the mission specifics.

As we train for and conduct missions, we are mindful that the maritime domain is a precious resource shared by the global community. We will conduct effective combat training, using live and simulated methods, while ensuring that we sustain our naval preeminence and our record of good environmental stewardship.

What We Provide the Nation

The Naval Service provides the Nation a multi-purpose team whose capabilities are applicable across the ROMO. While most frequently employed to *prevent* conflict, we are manned, trained and equipped to *prevail* in combat. We provide:

- **Persistent presence,** operating forward while respecting the sovereignty of others. Naval forces conduct military engagement and security cooperation to build partnerships; prevent and deter conflict; communicate our Nation's intent; conduct crisis response and limited contingency operations; and when necessary, facilitate the introduction of additional naval, joint, or multinational forces, as well as interagency, multinational, or non-governmental organizations.

- **Self-sustaining, sea-based expeditionary forces,** the Nation's preeminent, combined-arms teams. Uniquely tailored to fight and win from the sea, we are manned, trained, equipped, and ready to operate without reliance on ports or airfields in an objective area. For the Naval Service, "expeditionary" is not limited to being "an armed force organized to accomplish a specific objective in a foreign country." Rather, *being* expeditionary is one of our defining characteristics—we are ready to fight when we "leave the pier," persistently forward postured, and self-sustaining throughout our deployments.

- *Maritime domain expertise,* fully cognizant of the complexities of the water, air, and land environments and their interfaces. We are the only force skilled at operating in this maneuver space. We fight by achieving access, establishing local sea control and projecting power ashore as part of a joint or multinational team. We effectively employ a range of lethal and non-lethal capabilities to counter both conventional and irregular challenges in the maritime domain as well as space and cyberspace.

- *Flexible force options,* scalable with respect to capability, capacity, and legal authorities. Our forward posture is a cost-effective means of proactively influencing events and responding to crises. When required, these naval forces can be rapidly reinforced by other naval forces surged[5] from globally dispersed locations. Our inherent mobility, organizational agility, and self-sustainability provide combatant commanders with a variety of options, including the ability to command and control joint task forces from afloat and ashore, across the ROMO.

- *Expanded deterrence,* through credible, maneuverable, forward deployed and scalable power projection capabilities—including ballistic missile defense and nuclear strike—and prevention activities that build capable partners and address the causes of instability and conflict.

- *Joint, multinational, and interagency enabling forces* that facilitate the integration and application of all elements of national power.

Naval operational maneuver is a great advantage of maritime powers, past and present...An amphibious force under way will move about five hundred nautical miles in a day...On land an army maneuvering at operational speed against weak opposition will advance about twenty-five statute miles a day. Concisely, in speed of operational movement ships have an order-of-magnitude advantage over an army...The introduction of aircraft and aerial logistics complicates this simplified description, but aircraft have never changed the threefold advantage of seapower...[6]

—Captain Wayne P. Hughes, Jr., USN (Retired), 2008
Senior Lecturer
Department of Operations Research
Naval Postgraduate School

Chapter 3

The Overarching Concept: The Sea as Maneuver Space

The objective should be to perform as far as practical the functions now performed on land at sea bases closer to the scene of operations…. This gives American power a flexibility and a breadth impossible of achievement by land-locked powers.[7]

—Samuel P. Huntington, 1954

Background

In the 21ˢᵗ century, information moves around the world almost instantaneously through cyberspace, and people and select goods quickly travel great distances by air. However, most materiel still moves the way it has for millennia—by sea. Ninety percent of the world's goods travel by sea. Similarly, whenever the United States conducts military operations on foreign soil, the vast majority of U.S. joint force materiel continues to be transported by sea.

Using *the sea as maneuver space* is the overarching concept of this publication. The Naval Service provides a sea-based force free from reliance on local ports and airfields. Naval forces continuously operate forward—and surge additional forces when necessary—to influence adversaries and project power.

Opportunity and Challenge

Previous generations found deploying joint forces and sustaining them overseas to be a hazardous undertaking. Adversaries, applying their own naval power, sought to deny our transit across the oceans or, failing that, our landing on the far shore. In the first half of the 20ᵗʰ century, U.S. Navy and Marine Corps leaders developed the capabilities necessary to establish sea control and project power ashore where and when desired. Following World War II however, the importance of these capabilities waned as the United States enjoyed extensive basing rights overseas, to include secure ports and airfields. This network of overseas bases has been significantly reduced since the end of the Cold War, even as the United States enters a new era characterized by a broad variety of strategic challenges that threaten its global influence. In addition to peer competitors with conventional and nuclear forces, the rise of non-state actors and the expansion of irregular challenges have dramatically increased the complexity of the security environment.

The ability to overcome diplomatic, geographic, and military impediments to access has re-emerged as a critical enabler for extending U.S. influence and projecting power overseas. As noted in the *Capstone Concept for Joint Operations* (CCJO):

> *The most likely occasions requiring the commitment of joint forces will arise, as they have for the past half-century, in places where few or no forces are permanently stationed. America's ability to project power rapidly and conduct and sustain operations globally thus will remain critically dependent on air and maritime freedom of movement and on sufficient strategic and operational lift.*[8]

Central Idea

The Naval Service uses the sea as maneuver space. Mobility and maneuverability constitute the Naval Service's primary operational attributes, stemming directly from the ability of naval forces to move long distances quickly and efficiently, and to maneuver within the maritime environment to achieve advantage in relation to an adversary.

Fully using the sea as maneuver space requires the:

- Ability to collect and share information to enhance global awareness of activities in the maritime domain.

- Ability to employ, support and sustain task-organized forces over extended ranges and durations to conduct diverse and often concurrent missions: engagement; relief and reconstruction; security; and combat operations.

- Capability and capacity to confront irregular challenges, especially in the littorals.

- Interoperable naval command and control (C2) capabilities that maintain due regard for national sovereignty, statutory responsibilities, and legal authorities among the various U.S. and international participants.

- Ability to be supported by, and to support, joint, interagency, and international partners through seabasing.

Global Awareness

Global awareness is a broad, non-doctrinal term referring to the knowledge and understanding required for decision-making across the range of military operations (ROMO). Today, it is being improved through the cumulative result of professional development, technological enhancements, and cooperative information sharing. Professional development includes expanding the regional and cultural awareness that allows Sailors, Marines, and Coast Guardsmen to accurately understand situations and take appropriate action in a prudent and timely manner. The persistent forward presence of naval forces contributes to regional understanding, which is further enhanced through both unilateral and multi-lateral operational experience. Every Sailor, Marine and Coast Guardsman is a collector and user of information. An increasingly linguistically diverse and culturally savvy force is improving our ability to interact with local populations, establish trust-based relationships, and inspire information sharing.

For the foreseeable future, global awareness will remain dependent upon the processing, exploitation, and dissemination of vast stores of collected data made available across global information networks. Today, this is increasingly accomplished through automation and advanced intelligence and information architectures. A key cooperative initiative to enhance global awareness is the national and international effort to improve maritime domain awareness (MDA). MDA is defined as "the effective understanding of anything associated with the maritime domain that could impact the security, safety, economy, or environment of a nation." Enhancing MDA depends primarily upon facilitating the sharing of information among partners, and increasing the compatibility of the related systems. Information must be exchanged among a diverse network of military, government, and international partners; as well as private sector and commercial participants. With this in mind, sharing information at the lowest classification level that the situation permits will offer the highest benefit in terms of gaining trust, broadening cooperation, and making comprehensive information available to the widest possible range of partners, decision makers, and tactical users.

Employing Task Organized Forces

Task-organizing is the act of establishing an operating force, support staff, or logistic package of specific size and composition to accomplish a unique task or mission. The Naval Service combines ships, personnel, equipment, and its other inherent capabilities—often with forces and units from allies, partners, and other government agencies—in an adaptive manner to provide the right force at the right time to achieve a particular operational objective.

Standard force packages comprised of units that train together prior to deploying overseas help the Naval Service respond effectively across the full range of military operations. Notionally, a carrier strike group consists of an aircraft carrier, carrier air wing, up to five surface combatants, a fleet oiler and a direct support submarine. An amphibious readiness group (ARG) normally consists of an amphibious assault ship (LHA or LHD), an amphibious transport dock (LPD) and a dock landing ship (LSD). In those cases when the amphibious assault ship does not contain a well deck, the ARG composition may be augmented to ensure that adequate well deck, vehicle square, and connector capacities are available. Independently deploying surface combatants and other units can join either of these force packages to create task groups with the capabilities necessary to secure the maritime maneuver space from air, subsurface or surface threats and accomplish the assigned mission. If necessary, whole force packages or task groups can be aggregated to create an expeditionary strike force (ESF) to support a large contingency operation or campaign. Generally, an ESF in support of the assault echelon of a single amphibious Marine expeditionary brigade (MEB) will total 17 amphibious ships; a second MEB would require the surging of all remaining U.S. Navy amphibious ships.

Effective aggregation of maritime forces relies on common tactics, techniques and procedures associated with intelligence, C2, fires, maneuver, logistics and force protection. This underscores the importance of sufficient joint and combined training, and of interoperable systems, to achieving and sustaining operational readiness. The Naval Service constantly seeks to sustain this critical foundation, to include allies and partners.

Once in theater, disaggregation of the standard force packages is the norm during peacetime operations. Smaller task organized action groups, down to individual units, are frequently established to conduct various combat missions as well as maritime security, maritime interdiction, security force assistance and humanitarian assistance and disaster response (HA/DR) missions within the assigned theater of operations. As a result, task organized force packages are increasingly being employed to complement the standard force packages, which also facilitates meeting the growing global demand for maritime forces. Navy and Marine component commanders and Coast Guard senior field commanders play a key role in this regard, requesting and employing tailored force packages to meet the combatant commanders' requirements.

Enhanced Marine Air-Ground Task Force Operations

The ability to use the sea as maneuver space is the critical design consideration for Marine capabilities. As "soldiers of the sea," the principal Marine Corps organization for all missions across the ROMO is the amphibious and expeditionary capable Marine air-ground task force (MAGTF). Task-organized to meet mission requirements, MAGTFs vary in size from several hundred to as many as 75,000 Marines and Sailors. All, however, are composed of at least four core elements under a single commander: a command element, an aviation combat element, a ground combat element, and a logistics combat element. Other Service or multinational forces may also be assigned or attached to a MAGTF to meet mission needs.

Since its inception, the MAGTF construct has proven itself highly flexible and adaptable. To ensure that future MAGTFs are equipped with the capabilities and capacities appropriate to the evolving security environment, the Marine Corps is exploring *enhanced MAGTF operations* (EMO). The EMO initiative is examining refinements to current tables of organization and equipment, as well as to select tactics, techniques, and procedures. These refinements seek to improve the ability of naval forces to: overcome challenges to access and mobility; employ, support, and sustain dispersed, subordinate maneuver units at extended distances or in compartmentalized terrain that creates physical separation from higher and adjacent units; interact effectively with local populations to understand a given situation and ensure that tactical actions support strategic goals; and perform engagement, relief and reconstruction, security and combat tasks in combination as appropriate to a given situation.

Mindful of the Marine Corps' enduring role as a naval, expeditionary force-in-readiness, the EMO initiative is driven by the premise that MAGTFs are primarily designed to be employed, supported and sustained from the sea. To operate from the sea, MAGTFs will be lean and agile—but still lethal.

Confronting Irregular Challenges

The Naval Service confronts irregular challenges at sea and in the littorals. Many of the threats in today's dynamic security environment are irregular in nature, arising from state and non-state actors that operate from an increasing number of poor, corrupt, lawless, or weakly governed areas in the world. They achieve psychological, economic, and political effects through criminal, insurgent, and terrorist activities that are perpetrated with the help of extended support networks, resilient C2 structures, illegal funding sources, and off-the-shelf technologies and arms. Globalization and readily available advanced information technologies are accelerating the growth of such unlawful actors and their organizations, and intensifying the global impact they can create.

Confronting irregular challenges within the maritime domain usually takes place as part of a comprehensive "whole of government" effort. Within that framework, the Naval Service supports U.S. government initiatives to help mitigate the causes of instability, improve governance, advance the rule of law and secure the flow of resources—frequently in concert with allies, partners, international organizations and non-governmental organizations.

General purpose forces conduct the full range of military operations to this end, including maritime security, counter-proliferation, security cooperation, security force assistance, stability, maritime interdiction, counter-insurgency and HA/DR missions. Frequently, the unique circumstances associated with confronting irregular challenges require general purpose forces to apply their capabilities in innovative ways, such as strike-fighters using their weapons systems as non-traditional intelligence, surveillance, and reconnaissance (ISR) sensors. The Naval Services are also rebalancing their capabilities to enhance their effectiveness against irregular threats. The Navy's Expeditionary Combat Command (NECC), for example, is particularly well suited to conduct riverine operations, construction, maritime security training and civil affairs tasks.

The Marine Corps has also developed a range of initiatives that enhance its general purpose forces' abilities to confront irregular challenges. Key among these are the Center for Irregular Warfare, the Center for Advanced Operational and Cultural Learning, the Security Cooperation Education and Training Center, the Marine Corps Information Operations Center, and the Marine expeditionary force staffs. The Marine Corps is also working with the Navy to establish force packages and combined training programs that will provide a tailorable "maritime raid capability" to address the diverse target sets that characterize irregular challenges.

The Coast Guard's Deployable Operations Group (DOG), comprised mostly of maritime safety and security teams with a special operations focus, brings together various specialized incident response, law enforcement and security teams into adaptive force packages for surge operations. Additionally, the Coast Guard has developed law enforcement detachments that enable U.S. Navy ships to conduct law enforcement operations, as well as train partner maritime forces to contribute effectively to the global effort to enhance maritime security.

19

Naval Command and Control
Command and control is the exercise of authority and direction by a properly designated commander over assigned and attached forces. Command and control functions are performed through an arrangement of personnel, equipment, communications, facilities, and procedures employed by a commander in planning, directing, coordinating, and controlling forces and operations in the accomplishment of the mission. Naval C2 relationships are based on a philosophy of centralized guidance, collaborative planning, and decentralized control and execution. With a long-standing practice of utilizing mission orders, naval C2 practices are intended to achieve relative advantage through organizational ability to observe, orient, decide and act. Mission orders enable continued operations in environments where communications are compromised or denied, allowing subordinates to exercise initiative consistent with the higher commander's intent.

The integrated application of naval capabilities across a diverse range of missions requires a flexible approach to command arrangements. Command relationship options include operational control, tactical control, or a "supported-supporting" relationship as described in Joint Publication 1 and are determined by the common superior commander, or establishing authority. Combat experience and the test of time have proven that the cooperative spirit of "supported-supporting" helps us optimize the effectiveness of all elements of the force. The type of relationship chosen by the establishing authority—usually a combatant commander—should be based on mission, authorities, nature and duration of the operation, force capabilities, C2 capabilities, operational environment, and recommendations from subordinate commanders.

Many 21st-century problems require solutions that involve the coordinated application of all elements of national power, often applied in concert with the efforts of multinational and non-governmental organizations. At present, however, interagency and multinational coordination lacks a formal process framework and supporting architecture. Naval forces must therefore be capable of collaboratively planning, preparing, executing, and assessing operations through innovative application of the related naval processes.

The Coast Guard is moving to improve interagency coordination in support of domestic port security through the *Interagency Operations Centers* (IOC) *Project*. This initiative is expanding the facilities and information systems within existing Sector Command Centers at high-priority ports so they can incorporate a multitude of diverse partners such as other law enforcement agencies, port authorities, and Department of Defense organizations. Designed to satisfy the mandates of the Security and Accountability for Every (SAFE) Port Act of 2006, the IOC Project incorporates the successful characteristics of several Coast Guard interagency pilot projects cited as models by the Act. At the operational level, the interface between the Coast Guard's IOC and the Navy's *maritime operations center* (MOC) must support information sharing, collaborative planning, coordination of supporting operations, and agile C2 transitions in response to items of interest that are approaching U.S. ports and coastal areas.

Navy's MOCs, established at all Navy component command headquarters, provide a common organizational framework through which Navy commanders exercise operational level C2. MOCs are functionally organized staffs that are trained, equipped and networked to support the commander's efficient and effective C2 of a joint force maritime component (JFMCC) or joint task force (CJTF). They are sized to command and control day-to-day peacetime theater security cooperation missions and exercises; maritime security missions including counter-proliferation, maritime interdiction, counter-terrorism, counter-piracy and other tasking related to irregular challenges; ISR, ballistic missile defense (BMD) and strike missions; and diverse crisis response operations. Additionally, the MOC's traditional hierarchy and organization is overlaid with collaborative cross-functional processes and is easily scalable to support the integrated planning, preparation, execution, and assessment required for major naval, joint, and multinational operations involving interagency, multinational and non-governmental organizations.

Marine expeditionary force (MEF) and Marine expeditionary brigade (MEB) commanders may be tasked to lead or form an operational level Service component, joint force functional component or CJTF command element. These Marine commanders are supported by readily deployable command elements that include the communications, intelligence, and expeditionary support capabilities necessary to establish fully functioning headquarters afloat, in austere locations ashore, or various combinations thereof. These expeditionary headquarters have demonstrated their ability to provide the nucleus of a joint or multinational command and to enable a variety of interagency and non-governmental organizations. Presently, Marine Corps component commanders have the ability to provide the nucleus of a joint or combined headquarters capable of commanding and controlling a range of operations, from major multi-lateral training exercises to combat, as well as coordinating noncombatant evacuation and major HA/DR efforts.

Seabasing

Seabasing is the deployment, assembly, command, projection, reconstitution, and re-deployment of joint power from the sea, without reliance on land bases within the operational area. It provides joint force commanders with the ability to conduct select functions and tasks at sea without dependence on infrastructure ashore. Seabasing has wide applicability across the ROMO—from *military engagement, security cooperation, and deterrence* activities to *crisis response and contingency operations,* to *major operations and campaigns.* It is a concept that employs a single ship, or task-organized mix of ships to achieve access and facilitate entry from the sea.

Naval Service seabasing supports not only naval, but also joint, interagency and multinational initiatives globally. The Naval Service continues to advance the capabilities that can be projected, sustained, supported, protected, and in some cases controlled, from the sea; but the full potential of seabasing is yet to be realized. For example, the current fleets of military sealift and merchant marine vessels that transport the preponderance of the joint force's materiel remain largely dependent upon secure ports near the objective area for offload. Building upon the seabasing foundation provided by surface combatants, aircraft carriers, amphibious ships, and military sealift ships, ongoing initiatives are focused on enhancing the Naval Service's capabilities to project task-organized forces at and from the sea. These capabilities include additional high-speed intra-theater lift, improved connectors that can transfer people and materiel at-sea,[9] enhanced maritime prepositioning,[10] and integrated naval logistics. These and other emerging initiatives will be employed in combination to reduce the joint force's reliance on ports in the operational area.

Seabasing is predicated on the ability to attain local maritime superiority. While a limited number of nations currently possess credible anti-access and area denial capabilities, naval forces are able to achieve sea control and sustain resilient sea-based operations in uncertain and hostile environments. Challenges to seabasing can also arise from coastal states that promulgate limitations on freedom of navigation based on their own environmental, conservation, immigration, sanitation, safety, customs, or security concerns. When directed, U.S. naval forces will challenge any restrictions that go beyond a coastal state's legitimate authority under international law.

Summary

Naval forces use the sea as maneuver space—the strategic concept embodied in *A Cooperative Strategy for 21st Century Seapower* (CS-21). To fully exploit the sea as maneuver space, naval forces leverage global awareness of activities in the maritime domain; the ability to employ scalable combat power in task-organized forces over extended ranges and durations; capability and capacity to confront irregular challenges; flexible naval command and control; and mission-tailored seabasing capabilities.

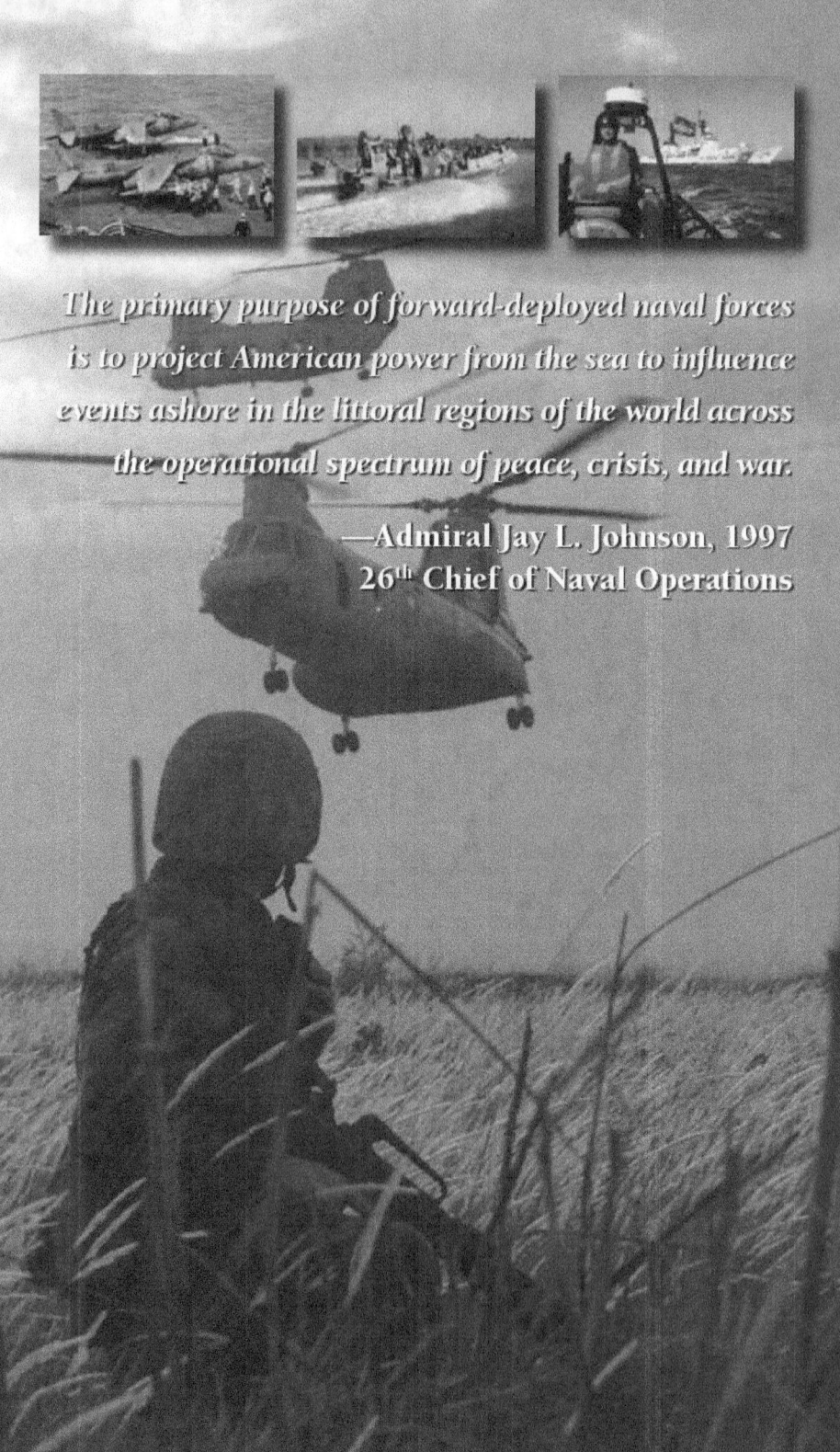

The primary purpose of forward-deployed naval forces is to project American power from the sea to influence events ashore in the littoral regions of the world across the operational spectrum of peace, crisis, and war.

—Admiral Jay L. Johnson, 1997
26th Chief of Naval Operations

Chapter 4
Forward Presence

The naval presence mission is simultaneously as sophisticated and sensitive as any, but also the least understood of all Navy missions. A well orchestrated naval presence can be enormously useful in complementing diplomatic actions to achieve political objectives. Applied deftly but firmly, in precisely the proper force, naval presence can be a persuasive deterrent to war. If used ineptly, it can be disastrous. Thus, in determining presence objectives, scaling forces, and appraising perceptions, there will never be a weapons system as important as the human intellect.

—Vice Admiral Stansfield Turner, USN, 1974
34th President of the Naval War College[11]

Background

The Naval Service has a long history of maintaining a forward naval presence in areas of vital interest to the United States. Originally conducted to protect U.S. merchant shipping, promote overseas trade, and support diplomacy, over time the basis of our forward presence operations has evolved and expanded to include crisis response as well as conventional and nuclear deterrence. Naval forward presence is a key element of the U.S. global defense posture. The complementary elements of this defense posture—sea-based, land-based, and the surface and air connectors between—support and sustain U.S. military operations throughout the globe.

The steady-state operations of sea-based naval forces enhance joint access by gaining familiarity with forward operating areas while also fostering the international relationships that may alleviate diplomatic impediments to access. They also provide the means to overcome geographic and, when necessary, military challenges to access. Forward postured naval forces deter adversaries; demonstrate U.S. commitment to our international partners; and respond rapidly to tension, coercion, crises and conflicts. Forward presence facilitates all other naval missions, most importantly sea control, which is a necessary condition for the deployment and sustained employment of any joint or multinational force.

Forward presence is achieved through a combination of forward stationed and rotationally deployed forces. **Forward stationed forces** are homeported overseas, where they conduct all training and most maintenance. The Navy and Marine Corps often refer to forward stationed units overseas as *forward deployed naval forces* (FDNF). The advantage of forward stationed naval forces is that they maximize continuous presence with a minimum number of ships. The benefits of forward stationing cannot be realized without host nation support from allies and friends—a circumstance that is not taken for granted by the Naval Service and that merits collaboration to ensure such arrangements are mutually beneficial. Forward stationed ships may require relief by rotationally deployed forces when entering shipyards for extended maintenance periods.

Rotationally deployed forces are based in the United States but regularly deploy overseas to maintain continuous presence in key regions. The advantage of rotationally deployed forces is that they can be employed without extensive overseas infrastructure, basing rights, or other host nation support. The disadvantage is that multiple ships are required in a training, maintenance, deployment cycle to sustain continuous presence. With due consideration for maintenance and training requirements, ships in the rotation may surge for short-duration activities between regularly scheduled deployments or in response to a crisis. Some forces—such as hospital ships, repair ships, or tenders—only deploy episodically to support specific operations.

Rotationally deployed ships complement forward stationed forces at main operating bases, forward operating sites, and cooperative security locations. The Naval Service maintains forward stationed personnel and resources in diverse locations overseas, such as Bahrain, Cuba, Diego Garcia, Greece, Guam, Italy, Japan, Korea, Norway, Singapore, and Spain. This global architecture enables economical naval and joint force deployment, employment and sustainment.

Critical enablers for U.S. forward naval forces are the combat logistics force ships and support ships operated by the Military Sealift Command (MSC). The combat logistics force includes the ships and helicopters that resupply combatant ships with fuel, food, parts, and ordnance while at sea, commonly termed "underway replenishment." They allow the fleet to remain underway for extended periods and to fully use the sea as maneuver space. Support vessels include command ships, fleet ocean tugs, rescue and salvage ships, hospital ships, ocean survey ships and joint high speed vessels. Collectively, these ships support continuous forward presence and the overseas operations of U.S. and allied naval forces. As such, they are essential to the success of *globally distributed* operations.

Opportunity and Challenge

The forward presence of naval forces serves to contain and deter regional adversaries while increasing the engagement opportunities with allies and partners to promote collective security, enhance global stability and confront irregular challenges. As the security environment evolves from unipolar to multi-polar with the emergence of numerous states with significant economic and military power, the importance of seamless interoperability with allies and effective coordination with partners cannot be overstated. The imperative to build and sustain partnerships that measurably contribute to maritime security, deterrence and combat effectiveness comes at a time when sensitivity to U.S. bases overseas is rising and the overall number of U.S. forces stationed on foreign soil is much lower than during the Cold War. In this context, sea-based forward presence provides the opportunity to conduct cooperative activities with allies and an expanding set of international partners, while minimizing the political, economic, cultural, and social impacts sometimes associated with forward stationed U.S. forces.

While forward, naval forces conduct planned activities focused on enhancing regional security and stability, such as security cooperation and security force assistance; maritime security operations; major training and readiness exercises; humanitarian and civic assistance; intelligence, surveillance, and reconnaissance (ISR); and information operations. These operations include allies and partners in bi-lateral and multi-lateral initiatives designed to address regional challenges and prepare for crisis response operations. The combatant commanders' demand for forward postured naval forces—particularly carrier strike groups (CSGs), amphibious ready groups with embarked Marine expeditionary units (ARG/MEUs), and surface action groups—exceeds the current and forecast capacity of the Naval Service. Since 2007 the combatant commanders' cumulative requests for naval forces have grown 29 percent for CSGs, 76 percent for surface combatants, 86 percent for ARG/MEUs, and 53 percent for individually deployed amphibious ships.[12]

The challenge is to employ *globally distributed, mission-tailored forces* across a wide range of missions that promote stability, prevent crises and combat terrorism; while maintaining the capability to *regionally concentrate credible combat power* to protect U.S. vital interests, assure friends, and deter and dissuade potential adversaries. Forward forces and forces surged from the United States, along with those of allies and partners, must be sufficiently ready and interoperable to respond effectively across a broad spectrum of crises.

Central Idea

Naval forces are ideally suited to shape and respond to the security challenges of the 21st century. The combination of forward stationed and rotationally deployed forces is a uniquely adaptable means to maintain global military presence while respecting the sovereignty of other nations. The presence of forward naval forces provides American policymakers with an expansive range of options to influence events and project power in peacetime, crisis, and war. These options are largely the result of interoperability with ally and partner maritime forces, achieved through effective, steady-state engagement activities; and the flexible employment of naval force packages that are tailored to specific capacity building, security cooperation or crisis response requirements.

Cooperative Action

The United States employs a "comprehensive" approach that focuses and synchronizes interagency efforts to promote good governance; the rule of law; social, economic and political development; stability; and global security. In this context, the Naval Service helps build partner capacity to maintain maritime security, respond to crises within the maritime domain, deter conflicts, and prevail in war. Building such capacity requires collaborative planning with partners—along with supporting regional allies and partners, international organizations, and non-governmental organizations—and a series of resulting activities that are conducted over time to achieve sustainable improvements. Naval forces provide the persistent forward presence necessary to support such initiatives, either in a leadership role, or in support of other U.S. entities, allies or partners better suited to lead the effort. Moreover, the ability to optimize the composition of the forward forces to meet the evolving needs of U.S. partners maximizes the return on investment from each event. Forward naval forces are similarly employed to enhance interoperability with allies, leading to more effective shaping of the security environment and response to crises.

Adaptive Force Packaging

Adaptive force packaging generates the *globally distributed, mission-tailored forces* required to resource the demands of the combatant commanders. The standard CSG and ARG force packages can be scaled up by incorporating additional ships; or disaggregated into smaller surface action groups or individual ships to conduct the full range of military operations, including capacity building, theater security cooperation (TSC) and combat operations. As global demands increase and TSC requirements become more refined, independently deploying units are frequently the best solution for many missions. In this regard, exploiting the inherent capability and flexibility of ships to fill non-traditional roles, such as the use of USNS maritime prepositioning ships for global fleet station, and high speed vessels for afloat staging base missions, is increasingly common.

Beyond innovatively employing every class of ship operated by the Naval Service, adaptive force packaging also includes tailoring the crew com-position and adding mission specific equipment to enhance effectiveness. For example, Marine detachments can be placed aboard large surface combatants, littoral combatants, and cutters to provide enhanced force protection; boarding and raiding capability; and mobile training teams. Similarly, cultural, language, law enforcement, legal, intelligence, and special operations experts can augment crews; and civil affairs, health services, construction engineering, and ISR capabilities such as SCAN EAGLE can be embarked and employed as required. Importantly, adap-tive force packaging is not constrained to ships—any capability or set of capabilities can be deployed and employed to accomplish an assigned mission—but the Naval Service is optimized to conduct expeditionary operations that are sustained from a sea base.

Forward Presence Force Posture

In the near term, forward presence force posture is necessarily shaped by ongoing commitments to Operations IRAQI FREEDOM and ENDURING FREEDOM. These commitments currently involve approximately 20,000 Marines conducting counterinsurgency, security cooperation, and civil-military operations in Afghanistan, plus another 2,000 Marines normally embarked on ships within the region. Also within the region are 24,000 Sailors at sea and ashore conducting maritime infrastructure protection, explosive ordnance disposal, combat construction engineering, cargo handling, combat logistics, maritime security operations, rule of law operations, riverine operations and other critical activities. Additionally, more than 400 Coast Guardsmen are conducting essential port operations, port and oil platform security, and maritime interception operations. The Naval Service commitments cited above also encompass more than 7,500 Individual Augmentees serving in a variety of joint or coalition billets.[13] As these operations unfold, the size and composition of committed naval forces will evolve, but long after the land component presence is reduced, naval forces will remain forward and present in the region.

For the foreseeable future, we will continue to maintain an FDNF CSG and ARG/MEU in the Western Pacific. We will also maintain continuous CSG and ARG/MEU presence in the Arabian Gulf/Indian Ocean and seek to deploy an additional ARG/MEU that will routinely shift between regions. Periodic aggregation of CSGs and ARG/MEUs into an expeditionary strike force will serve to demonstrate and sustain the proficiency to operate effectively as a large maneuver force. Whether forward stationed or rotationally deployed, these naval forces are present to protect U.S. vital interests, assure its friends, and deter and dissuade potential adversaries.

The evolving security environment invites increased presence in the Mediterranean Sea. Likely tasks include, but are not limited to, surveillance, maritime security, counter-proliferation, noncombatant evacuation, humanitarian assistance and disaster response (HA/DR), and sea-based integrated air and ballistic missile defense (IAMD) operations. Naval forces present in the Mediterranean can also respond immediately to emergent crises and rapidly reinforce other naval and joint forces in the Arctic Ocean, Black Sea, Arabian Gulf, Indian Ocean, and along the west coast of Africa. To support similar responsiveness throughout the balance of the world, surface ships, attack submarines, and guided missile submarines will rotationally deploy to meet combatant commander and other national tasking.

In support of geographic combatant commanders' long-term TSC and global maritime partnership (GMP) engagement missions, episodic *global fleet stations* (GFS) will be established in regions such as the Arabian Gulf, Southeast Asia, the Caribbean Basin, the Gulf of Guinea, and the Horn of Africa. The *Global Fleet Station Concept of Operations* defines GFS as "a highly visible, positively engaged, persistent sea base of operations from which to interact with partner nation military and civilian populations and the global maritime community." This interaction will be conducted by a combination of Navy, Marine Corps, and Coast Guard personnel, in concert with joint, interagency and international partners. GFS are supported by a combination of platforms such as amphibious ships with embarked special purpose Marine air-ground task forces (SP MAGTFs), maritime prepositioning ships, support vessels, and surface combatants, which together possess surface and vertical lift capability, endurance, space for a variety of detachments and equipment, and the ability to operate at the sea-land interface.

To further support the combatant commanders' TSC and maritime security efforts, high- and medium-endurance cutters will be rotationally deployed to maintain a presence in Mediterranean/African littoral waters and the Western Pacific/Indian Ocean, as well as the Caribbean Basin and Eastern Pacific. Additionally, law enforcement detachment (LEDET) teams and port security units (PSUs), in combination with other naval forces, will continue to enhance the combatant commanders' capability to conduct the full spectrum of naval missions, especially in the littorals. LEDETs consist of active duty personnel who operate onboard U.S. and partner nation naval vessels in order to provide expanded law enforcement authority, expertise and capability to carry out interdiction and apprehension operations from U.S. and partner nation surface assets. LEDETs also provide partnership capacity through support and information exchange among joint, allied and partner nation maritime forces.[14] PSUs are deployable Coast Guard reserve units organized for sustained port security. They provide waterside protection and layered defense of key assets such as: pier areas, high value units, and harbor entrances at the termination or origination point of the sea lines of communication (SLOCs).[15]

Many nations, including the United States, have national security interests in the Arctic. The Naval Service is prepared to operate in this unique and harsh environment, either independently or in conjunction with other nations. However, the lack of environmental awareness, navigation capabilities, and supporting infrastructure, as well as competing jurisdictional and resource claims, are significant challenges that must be overcome by naval forces. At a minimum, this will require the episodic deployment of submarines, icebreakers or ice-capable ships to the Polar Regions, as well as increased investments in icebreaking capabilities and associated technologies.

Summary

The Naval Service employs *globally distributed, mission-tailored forces* to accomplish a wide range of missions that promote stability, prevent crises, and combat terrorism; while maintaining the capability to *regionally concentrate credible combat power* to protect U.S. vital interests; assure its friends; and deter, dissuade, and if necessary, defeat potential adversaries. Persistent forward presence, generated through a combination of forward stationed and rotationally deployed naval forces, provides American policymakers with an expansive range of options to shape and respond to the security challenges of the 21st century.

Many of today's maritime threats come from non-State actors that do not respect national borders, are not military in nature, and seek to blend into the normal course of legitimate activity in the maritime domain. Criminal actors are constantly learning, adapting and growing as they use the vastness of the oceans to their advantage, cloak themselves within the anonymity afforded to most maritime activities, exploit advances of globalization, and flourish in weak coastal States with poor governance.

—Admiral Thad Allen, USCG, 2007
23rd Commandant of the Coast Guard

Chapter 5
Maritime Security

Naval power is the natural defense of the United States.

—President John Adams, 1796
2nd President of the United States

Background

As a maritime nation, the United States is dependent upon the sea for both national security and economic prosperity. The Nation is geographically blessed and bounded by two great oceans that have historically protected us from external threats and enabled us to garner the world's resources and engage in the global markets. The safety and economic interests of the United States, its allies and partners critically depend upon the unimpeded trade and commerce that traverse the world's oceans. Consequently, U.S. vital national interests are tied to a secure maritime environment, which in turn places global responsibilities upon the Naval Service.

Maritime security is a non-doctrinal term defined as those tasks and operations conducted to protect sovereignty and maritime resources, support free and open seaborne commerce, and to counter maritime-related terrorism, weapons proliferation, transnational crime, piracy, environmental destruction, and illegal seaborne immigration. Effective maritime security requires a comprehensive effort to promote global economic stability and protect legitimate ocean-borne activities from hostile or illegal acts in the maritime domain. In addition to security operations along the U.S. coastline, globally-distributed naval forces conducting maritime security operations contribute to homeland defense in depth.

Maritime security may be divided into *individual* or *collective* categories. *Individual* maritime security operations involve actions taken by a single nation-state to provide for its safety and security, consistent with its rights. While the responsibility and capacity of individual nations to secure their territorial waters is the foundation upon which global maritime security is built, *A Cooperative Strategy for 21ˢᵗ Century Seapower* (CS-21) notes that unilateral action by a single nation cannot ensure the security of the global maritime commons: *collective* maritime security operations are required to unite actions of like-minded nation-states to promote mutual safety and security at sea.

Opportunity and Challenge

The size and complexity of the maritime commons create unique security challenges for the international community as terrorists and criminals leverage the easily accessible, largely unregulated expanse of the maritime domain to mask and facilitate their illicit activities. Threats to safety and security include piracy, narcotics smuggling, human trafficking, weapons proliferation, environmental destruction, and the pilfering of natural resources. Identifying, tracking, and neutralizing these threats is essential to U.S. national security and the global economy.

The sea is vast, the littorals extensive, and the threats to U.S. interests are varied, determined, and persistent. These conditions cannot be sufficiently shaped by the Naval Service alone, and demand that America partner with nations that share its interest in global maritime security and the prosperity it underpins.

Central Idea

Global maritime security can only be achieved through the integration of national and regional maritime cooperation, awareness and response initiatives. To this end, unprecedented coordination among governments, the private sector, and multinational organizations including naval and maritime security forces, law enforcement agencies, customs and immigration officials, masters of vessels and other merchant mariners, shipping companies, and port operators is required. The Naval Service plays a critical role in facilitating this coordination, and is uniquely manned, trained and equipped to help allies and partners develop the maritime professionals, infrastructure, awareness and response capabilities that are a prerequisite for maritime security. The Nation's *globally distributed, mission-tailored naval forces* not only conduct the full range of related operations—from unilateral assistance at sea, law enforcement and maritime interception operations to multinational counter-piracy operations—they help willing allies and partners build the capacity, proficiency and interoperability to do the same.

Increased Cooperation

The United States has numerous maritime law enforcement treaties and security arrangements to address various maritime security challenges, including drug interdiction, migrant interdiction, counter-piracy, fisheries enforcement, and proliferation security. Each agreement is unique and tailored to requirements, diplomatic and political relationships, and the domestic laws and policies of the participating nations. These agreements expand U.S. maritime authority and eliminate border seams that are exploited by illicit actors. As transnational maritime threats evolve, the Naval Service will continue to collaborate with the requisite U.S. authorities to develop any additional arrangements with foreign partners that are required to achieve maritime security. The Naval Service also supports mechanisms that underpin maritime security, including organizations such as the International Maritime Organization (IMO) that has instituted vessel tracking, vessel and port security measures, and strengthened the Convention on Suppression of Unlawful Acts at Sea (SUA); international law including the U.N. Convention on the Law of the Sea; regional, multinational, and bilateral agreements; domestic laws and regulations; and private-sector practices and procedures.

Within the U.S. Government, the Naval Service is a key stakeholder in the Maritime Operational Threat Response (MOTR) plan, which establishes protocols that facilitate coordinated, unified, timely, and effective planning and execution by the various agencies that have maritime responsibilities. Lead and supporting agencies are based on the location of the threat, existing law, desired outcome, magnitude of the hazard, response capabilities required, asset availability and authority to act. This interagency approach builds upon the unique contributions of each entity to respond to a full range of maritime security threats, including terrorism, and establishes the procedures to coordinate actions that frequently support a tactical response by the Naval Service. The Navy and Coast Guard, in accordance with the *National Fleet* policy, integrate their multi-mission platforms, infrastructure, and personnel to generate force packages tailored for specific maritime security responses and missions. This practice allows each Service to leverage the unique capabilities of the other, as part of a joint task force thousands of miles from the United

States, or in response to operational tasking close to home in support of civil authorities. The increasing commonality between Navy and Coast Guard systems, including radars, antennas, deck guns, airframes and unmanned systems, has improved both interoperability and sustainability during joint maritime security operations.

The responsibility of individual nations to maintain maritime security within their waters is the foundation upon which global maritime security is built. U.S. allies and partners possess capabilities that range from limited port or coastal maritime security forces to major navies with potent sea control and power projection capabilities. U.S. naval forces, in accordance with combatant commander theater security cooperation (TSC) plans, collaborate with allies and partners alike to develop the expertise, infrastructure, awareness, and capacity to respond to the full range of maritime security threats and irregular challenges.

Maritime Security Force Assistance (MSFA)

MSFA comprises efforts to strengthen security burden-sharing with foreign military and civilian maritime security forces and government institutions, as well as multinational and regional maritime security entities. These activities assist partner naval forces to become more proficient at providing security to their populations. In the context of the global maritime commons, MSFA promotes stability by developing partner nation capabilities to govern, control, and protect their harbors, inland and coastal waters, natural resources, commercial concerns, and national and regional maritime security interests. MSFA activities are conducted across the range of military operations (ROMO) and during all phases of military operations, in coordination with U.S. government agencies and in support of larger U.S. policy goals. Many of the Coast Guard's statutory missions align with foreign partner emerging demand to proactively deal with increasing threats to their sovereignty and resources. Geographic combatant commanders' (GCC) theater campaign plans and security cooperation initiatives are evolving to encompass combined Navy and Coast Guard capabilities tailored to develop competencies of host nation maritime security forces. Often these nations do not possess the requisite assets and tactics to self-police. Navy ships, Coast Guard cutters coupled with complementary law enforcement detachments (LEDETs) and training teams are ideal instruments of soft power to effect national objectives.

MSFA initiatives foster trust and interoperability with allies and enduring partners, increase capabilities and capacities to address conventional and irregular threats, reduce the ungoverned areas within the maritime domain, promote regional stability, and set conditions that dissuade disruptive acts through cooperative actions. Expeditionary operations, enduring partnership missions, as well as bilateral and multi-lateral exercises involving nearly every Naval Service capability comprise the most common MSFA initiatives.

Fleet and Expeditionary Operations

Naval forces will often conduct MSFA concurrent with other forward operations. For example, while conducting security patrols around the Iraqi off-shore oil platforms, Navy and Coast Guard maritime security forces integrated Iraqi military personnel into the operation to improve their expertise and proficiency. Similarly, while maintaining port and waterway security, Coast Guard port security unit (PSU) and Navy maritime expeditionary security squadron members trained Iraqi naval forces on point and perimeter security defense operations under the supervision of the Iraq Training and Advisory Mission. As general purpose forces embarked on naval vessels, Marines also conducted MSFA with coalition and partner nation naval forces. In these cases, Naval Service personnel benefited from the MSFA activities as well, gaining a greater understanding of local customs and conditions, which enhanced their effectiveness.

Likewise, Coast Guard cutters and LEDETs—active duty Coast Guard personnel employed on partner nation naval vessels in order to provide expanded law enforcement authority, expertise and capability to carry out interdiction and apprehension operations—frequently provide technical assistance to foreign law enforcement partners. Cutter boarding teams and LEDETs instruct, demonstrate and assist with searches, and evidence testing and processing. MSFA, in the form of advanced boarding procedure training, is increasingly requested by coalition partners and has reduced the risk associated with counter-piracy operations off Somalia. Additionally, the Coast Guard's International Port Security (IPS) program assesses the effectiveness of anti-terrorism measures in the ports of U.S. trading partners pursuant to a U.S. statutory requirement. This form of MSFA evaluates countries' implementation of the International Ship and Port Facility Security (ISPS) Code, shares maritime security "best practices," and makes recommendations for improvement.

Enduring, Rotational Maritime Partnership Missions

The global fleet station concept has given rise to a variety of enduring capacity-building activities that are supported by mission-tailored rotational forces. The Africa Partnership Station (APS) initiative exemplifies the rigorous, holistic approach to enhancing maritime security that the Naval Service employs around the world. Beginning with a specific maritime security condition to be achieved, for example "trafficking is stopped through western Africa," individual *country action plans* are collaboratively developed with the littoral countries to build the cadre of maritime professionals, maritime security infrastructure, maritime domain awareness, and maritime security force response capability necessary to achieve the objective condition. The country action plans integrate and synchronize supporting activities by other U.S. government entities, as well as those of allies, other partners, international organizations, and non-governmental organizations that share a common interest in achieving the maritime security condition. The detailed planning that is the foundation of this approach facilitates resourcing the initiative, avoids duplication of effort among international stakeholders, and drives the long-term scheduling of rotational forces to maximize progress by the partner. Moreover, the synchronization of related country action plans through a *regional action plan* that establishes enabling capabilities such as *regional coordination centers*, serves to establish a regional capacity that is invariably required to achieve measurable improvements in maritime security. To this end, Naval Service capabilities are employed in both supported and supporting roles, and typically conduct training events, exercises, and combined operations with numerous partners during a single deployment. For example, a subset of APS includes the African Maritime Law Enforcement Partnership (AMLEP), in which Navy warships, Coast Guard cutters, and partner vessels with embarked Coast Guard LEDETs and mobile training teams (MTTs) conduct operations and professional exchanges to advance maritime security and law enforcement competencies. The character of such activities and required capabilities vary depending on the security enhancement sought—from protection of ports, off-shore infrastructure, undersea resources or the environment to the interdiction of illegal fishing, piracy, narcotics smuggling, human trafficking, and weapons proliferation—but the first principle for successful maritime partnership missions is a steadfast focus on planned activities that make progress toward the specific maritime security condition to be achieved.

Fleet and Regional Exercises and Training

Bilateral and multi-lateral exercises serve to increase the proficiency, interoperability and confidence of U.S. naval forces and those of its allies and partners across the entire ROMO. Such exercises incorporate tailored training objectives to address the needs of the maritime security forces involved, from fundamental competencies such as basic naval seamanship to the most technically complex aspects of naval warfare such as ballistic missile defense, amphibious assault and undersea warfare. Exercises also bring together nations that otherwise would not conduct combined operations. Major maritime exercises include: Rim of the Pacific (RIMPAC), the largest combined exercise in the Pacific; Cooperation Afloat Readiness and Training (CARAT); Southeast Asia Cooperation Against Terrorism (SEACAT); Annual Exercise (ANNUALEX) with Japan; FOAL EAGLE in Korea; Baltic Operations Exercise (BALTOPS); and UNITAS, PANAMAX, and TRADEWINDS in the Western Hemisphere. All of these exercises involve ships, aircraft, and personnel ashore to conduct MSFA, ultimately improving the ability of U.S. naval forces to respond effectively to regional security threats in concert with its allies and partners.

Enhanced Awareness

Comprehensive maritime domain awareness (MDA) is the foundation of global maritime security. MDA requires an architecture that collects, fuses, analyzes and disseminates enormous quantities of classified and unclassified information regarding vessels, people, cargo, infrastructure, maritime areas of interest, and ongoing maritime security operations. The contributions of forward postured, persistent and culturally aware naval forces are critical, but not sufficient, to achieve comprehensive MDA. In fact, the combined efforts of the world's naval forces—if they could be aligned through military-to-military relationships—would still be insufficient. Comprehensive MDA can only be achieved through the seamless collaboration of the entire maritime community—naval forces, maritime-related organizations, the shipping industry, insurance companies, and mariners of every ilk. The Naval Service is responsible for facilitating such collaboration among the naval forces of allies and partners as a matter of first priority, and among the balance of the maritime community secondarily.

The basic objective of MDA initiatives is to discern who owns, operates, and controls a vessel; what activity is being conducted by the vessel; when will the activity be conducted; where will the activity be conducted; why the activity is being conducted; and how illegal activities are being concealed. To this end, collaboration correctly begins with the sharing of information available from existing systems, such as shore-based, ship-borne, and airborne radar systems, to build a common operating picture (COP). A comprehensive, real-time COP is considered as important for safe, effective maritime operations as clearly defined command and control relationships. Additional information to augment the basic radar COP can be gleaned from a variety of public databases and systems such as the Automatic Identification System (AIS). Similar to aircraft identification transponders, AIS is a protocol adopted by the International Maritime Organization to automatically share unclassified ship identification, safety of navigation and voyage information between AIS users operating in proximity to each other. This data is collected and fused with geospatial and oceanographic data to create increasingly comprehensive maritime domain awareness that can be shared with other U.S. agencies, allies and partners. The U.S. Coast Guard's National AIS (NAIS) project, which collects data from AIS-equipped surface vessels in the Nation's territorial waters and adjacent seas out to 2,000 nautical miles, is a conduit for maritime domain information that supports both Naval Service and international operations.

Response Operations

U.S. naval forces, often in concert with joint general purpose and special operations forces, other government agencies, and international partners, actively respond to conventional and irregular maritime threats. Naval Service response operations include:

- **Increased Surveillance and Tracking.** Vessels of interest are subject to increased surveillance and tracking, using a wide variety of military and commercial space-based systems, as well as air, surface, and underwater sensors. These actions facilitate more efficient, effective interdiction operations and are increasingly conducted by long-range, extended-endurance unmanned platforms with multi-spectral sensors.

- **Combined Task Force (CTF) Operations.** U.S. naval forces, in conjunction with allies and partners, will continue to conduct combined operations to counter specific maritime security threats such as piracy, smuggling and weapons trafficking. For example, the multinational task force CTF 151 was established in January 2009 to conduct counter-piracy operations in the Gulf of Aden and Somali basin.

■ *Maritime Interception Operations (MIO).* MIO monitor, query, and board merchant vessels to enforce sanctions against other nations such as those embodied in United Nations Security Council Resolutions and prevent the transport of restricted goods. Boarding teams comprised of Sailors, Marines, Coast Guardsmen and other law enforcement personnel are trained in visit, board, search, and seizure techniques and conduct specific missions in accordance with relevant authorities, laws, jurisdictions and capabilities.

■ *Law Enforcement Operations.* Law enforcement operations (LEO) are a form of interception operations distinct from MIO. Coast Guard cutters frequently conduct independent LEO while exercising Title 14 authority in deep water and littoral environments. U.S. Navy and foreign naval vessels routinely embark Coast Guard LEDETs and shift tactical control to the Coast Guard while conducting LEO.

■ *Expanded Maritime Interception Operations.* Expanded MIO (EMIO) are authorized by the President and directed by the Secretary of Defense to intercept vessels identified to be transporting terrorists and/or terrorist-related materiel that pose an imminent threat to the United States and its allies.[16]

Summary

Global maritime security can only be achieved through the coordinated activities of governments, the private sector, and multinational organizations including naval and maritime security forces, law enforcement agencies, customs and immigration officials, and the maritime community writ large. The Naval Service plays a critical role in facilitating this coordination, and is uniquely manned, trained and equipped to help allies and partners develop the maritime professionals, infrastructure, awareness and response capabilities that are a prerequisite for maritime security. U.S. *globally distributed, mission-tailored naval forces* effectively conduct the full range of maritime security operations and are instrumental in building the capacity, proficiency and interoperability of partners and allies that share our aspiration to achieve security throughout the maritime commons.

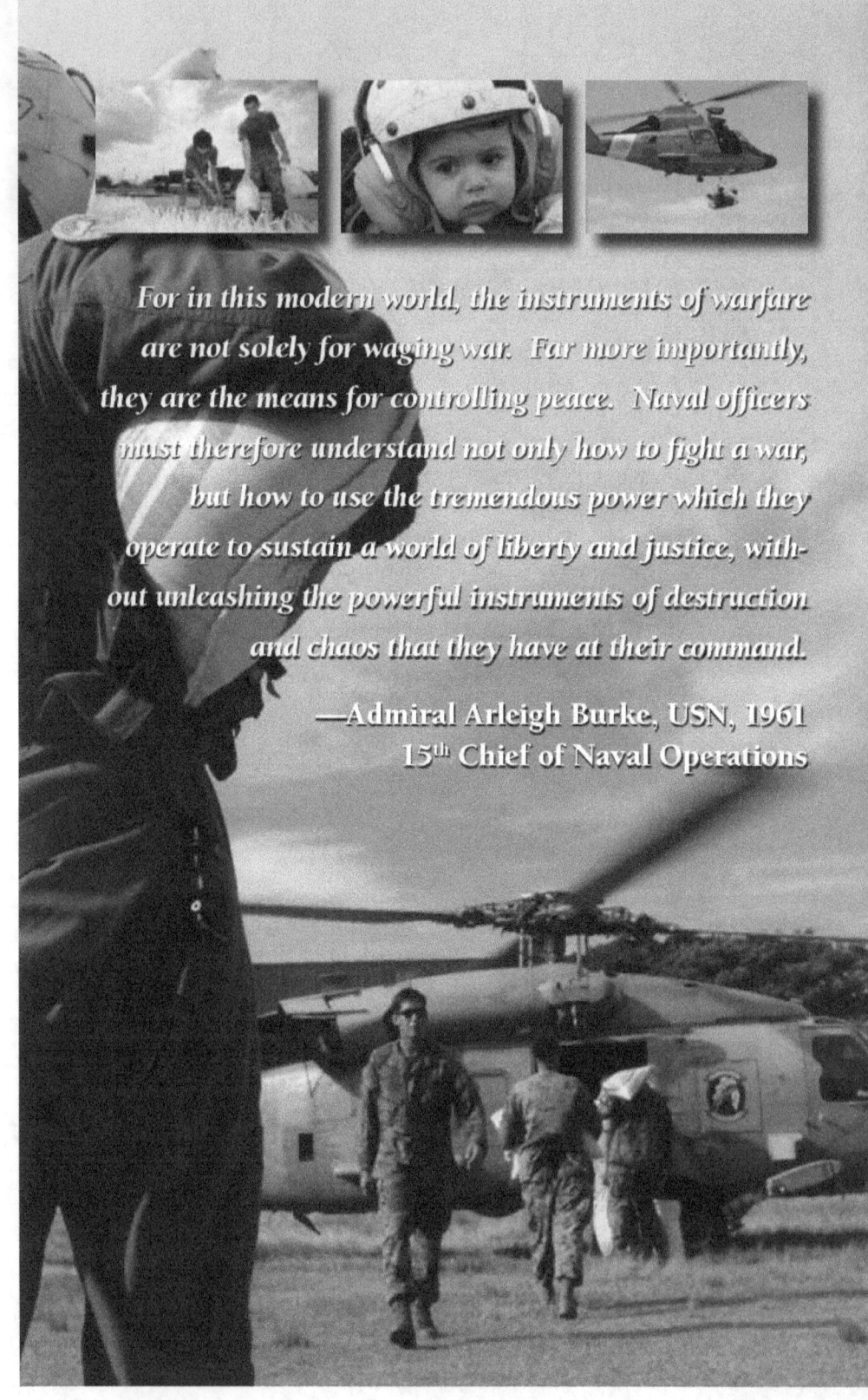

For in this modern world, the instruments of warfare are not solely for waging war. Far more importantly, they are the means for controlling peace. Naval officers must therefore understand not only how to fight a war, but how to use the tremendous power which they operate to sustain a world of liberty and justice, without unleashing the powerful instruments of destruction and chaos that they have at their command.

—Admiral Arleigh Burke, USN, 1961
15th Chief of Naval Operations

Chapter 6

Humanitarian Assistance and Disaster Response

During the nineteenth and most of the twentieth centuries, the very thought that sea powers might regularly use naval platforms to deliver humanitarian aid, as opposed to cutting off and starving an enemy's supply lines, would have seemed alien. In the twenty-first century, however, national power and prestige are more and more characterized by "soft power." UNIFIED ASSISTANCE showed that "hard power" assets like aircraft carriers can also be the best providers of "soft power."[17]

—Bruce A. Elleman, *Waves of Hope*, 2007
Naval Historian

Background

On 26 December 2004 major portions of Southeast Asia were ravaged by a tsunami, a broad-ranging catastrophe that impacted thousands of communities and directly affected nine countries. Within days U.S. naval forces from around the globe were mobilized to provide aid. III Marine Expeditionary Force (III MEF) was designated as the command element for Combined Support Force 536 to conduct Operation UNIFIED ASSISTANCE. Twenty-two U.S. ships, including the ABRAHAM LINCOLN Carrier Strike Group, BONHOMME RICHARD Expeditionary Strike Group, USS ESSEX, USS FORT MCHENRY with a special purpose MAGTF, USCGC MUNRO, USNS JOHN MCDONNELL and six maritime prepositioning ships were diverted from their scheduled routes to render aid that included subsistence, medical support, engineering support, port hydrographic surveys and extensive debris removal. U.S. naval forces did not work in isolation; their immediate response evolved into a multifaceted effort that included other Services, other agencies, the U.S. Agency for International Development (USAID), other countries, non-governmental organizations (NGOs), and private volunteer organizations.

Naval Service capabilities to establish maritime security and project combat power have repeatedly proven effective at responding to major disasters. From 1970 through 2000, U.S. forces were involved in 366 humanitarian missions, a number made more significant when compared to the 22 combat-related missions during the same period.[18] In recent years, U.S. naval forces have responded to an earthquake in Pakistan, Hurricane Katrina on the U.S. Gulf Coast, typhoons in the Philippines, a mudslide on the island of Leyte, a hurricane in Nicaragua, cyclones in Bangladesh, and a bridge collapse in the United States. Even more recently, naval forces deployed to provide leading support to disaster relief operations following the earthquake that devastated Haiti. These forces included the aircraft carrier USS CARL VINSON, USS BATAAN ARG/22nd MEU, USS NASSAU ARG/24th MEU, USNS COMFORT, NECC personnel, PSU 307, USCGC FORWARD, HAMILTON, OAK, MOHAWK, TAHOMA and VALIANT, and more than twenty other U.S. ships.

Operating without reliance on ports and airfields ashore, and in possession of organic medical support, strategic and tactical lift, logistics support, robust communications capabilities and premier planning and coordination tools, both *globally-distributed* and *regionally concentrated* naval forces are ideally suited for "humanitarian assistance and disaster response" (HA/DR) in the littorals where the preponderance of the world's population resides. Usually performed in support of U.S. government partners, HA/DR activities include, but are not limited to, defense support to civil authorities, humanitarian and civic assistance, foreign humanitarian assistance, foreign disaster relief, foreign assistance, humanitarian evacuation, development assistance, maritime environmental response operations, and selected aspects of security assistance, in accordance with their doctrinal definitions.

Opportunity and Challenge

The world population has been migrating to the littorals, creating a situation in which episodic natural or man-made disasters have greater potential to cause catastrophic human suffering. Both *globally distributed* and *regionally concentrated* naval forces will continue to be called upon to conduct HA/DR operations, either in the lead or in support of an international effort. Additionally, geographic combatant commanders are increasingly employing humanitarian assistance proactively to promote safety, security, and stability. Both proactive and reactive HA/DR efforts are undertaken alongside the host nation; other participating nations;

multinational, regional, and non-governmental organizations; and in close coordination with counterparts at the Department of State, USAID and other federal agencies. The challenge to U.S. naval forces is to enhance their ability to conduct HA/DR without degrading naval forces' capability and proficiency to conduct more traditional naval missions. Given their forward presence, inherent mobility and flexible capabilities, U.S. naval forces are frequently the "force of choice" for such missions. However, the demands of emergent, reactive HA/DR can affect readiness, logistical sustainment and operational dwell, and often require contingency funding in order to reset those units involved.

Central Idea

HA/DR is a core capability. Proactive HA/DR activities employ U.S. *globally distributed, mission-tailored naval forces* to address ally and partner needs that may not be directly related to national security, but they reflect the values and desires of the American people to render aid and reduce suffering. In so doing, these activities enhance or restore critical host nation capacity, provide an opportunity to engage with a broader cross-section of the host nation's population, and build relationships that serve to increase trust. Activities undertaken during reactive HA/DR have a similar effect, but the often extreme circumstances and severe risks to the population that characterize such events demand an immediate response that can only be provided by expeditionary naval forces trained and proficient in diverse crisis response operations.

Proactive HA/DR

Enduring, rotational missions like PACIFIC PARTNERSHIP and CONTINUING PROMISE build critical partner capacity and improve disaster response readiness through training and the development of habitual relationships with relevant partner ministries, departments and officials. Such global maritime partnership initiatives, along with special purpose Marine air-ground task forces (SP MAGTFs) formed to conduct security cooperation activities, complement other joint, interagency, international and NGO efforts that leverage their own unique skills, expertise, and host nation contacts. The day-to-day coordination of Naval Service, joint, interagency, international and NGO proactive HA/DR efforts sets conditions for effective collaboration when an in-extremis response is required.

Reactive HA/DR

Reactive HA/DR operations not only meet the urgent needs of the partner, they enhance Naval Service mission readiness across the full range of military operations. Usually requiring only modest adjustments to how naval forces are organized, deployed, and employed, reactive HA/DR operations pose the same challenges to naval forces as those encountered during security related crisis response operations. Employing expeditionary naval capabilities—intelligence, surveillance, and reconnaissance (ISR), maneuverability, sustainability, lift, medical care, construction engineering, and more—combined with planning and command and control (C2) proficiency; joint and interagency protocols; habitual military-to-military and political-military relationships with partners; and growing relationships with other international and non-governmental organizations; the Naval Service is uniquely suited to respond to disasters and to provide humanitarian assistance across a broad range of circumstances. Formal C2, supported/supporting, and coordination relationships with the responding entities will be rapidly established to ensure that the responsible authority possesses the latitude and wherewithal to meet the unique demands of the crisis. In this regard, the Naval Service will be mindful of the host nation's sovereignty and will respond with due regard for the host nation's desires and the U.S. lead agency's direction.

The Naval Service has staged critical HA/DR supplies on select ships, and prepositioned larger quantities at forward locations around the world, including Souda Bay in the Mediterranean, Diego Garcia in the Indian Ocean and Guam in the Western Pacific. This posture reduces the response time for reactive HA/DR missions and permits the Naval Service to better leverage the flexibility of globally dispersed, mission-tailored forces.

Summary

In today's globally connected world, news of humanitarian crises and natural or man-made disasters is reported almost immediately. Although the primary focus of naval forces remains combat effectiveness, their multi-mission capabilities allow those same forces to provide rapid assistance that can mitigate human suffering and restore critical partner capacity.

Events of October 1962 indicated, as they had all through history, that control of the sea means security. Control of the seas can mean peace. Control of the seas can mean victory. The United States must control the seas if it is to protect your security...

—**President John F. Kennedy, 1963**
35th President of the United States

Chapter 7
Sea Control

*As long as the sea is at our gates, North America will remain
the last great island. Her strategy, if she is to win and survive,
must be maritime...America's safety and well-being depend in
primary measure upon American ability to control and, even
more important, to exploit control of the seas.[19]*

—Colonel Robert D. Heinl, USMC, 1962
Military Historian and Defense Journalist

Background
Throughout U.S. history, control of the sea has been a precursor for
victory in war and prosperity in peace. Sea control is the essence of seapower—it allows naval forces to close within striking distance of land to
neutralize land-based threats to maritime access, which in turn enhances
freedom of action at sea and the resulting ability to project power ashore.
The interrelationship between sea control and power projection mandates
that the Naval Service possess capabilities and capacity to concurrently
shape conditions in the maritime, space and cyberspace domains,
sufficient to accomplish the Nation's defense strategy.

The vastness of the world's oceans makes it impossible for the Naval
Service to achieve global sea control. The combatant commanders'
operational objectives, the strategic maritime geography, and the capabilities of potential adversaries drive the scale of forward naval presence
and surge capability necessary to conduct effective local and regional
sea control operations. Such operations against a capable adversary
cannot be wholly conducted from the sea—they will require the support
of land-based aircraft for intelligence, surveillance, and reconnaissance
(ISR), undersea warfare, and aerial refueling. In this context, sea control
operations are:

The employment of naval forces, supported by land and air forces as appropriate, in order to achieve military objectives in vital sea areas. Such operations include destruction of enemy naval forces, suppression of enemy sea commerce, protection of vital sea lanes, and establishment of local military superiority in areas of naval operations.

While major battles to achieve sea control have not occurred since World War II, freedom of navigation and global maritime commerce are threatened every day by state and non-state actors who disrupt legal activities in the maritime domain and conduct piracy on the high seas. Moreover, deployment of joint forces and their sustainment during crisis response operations and land-centric conflicts is dependent on secure sea lines of communication. As a result, naval forces will for the foreseeable future conduct sea control operations to enforce freedom of navigation, sustain unhindered global maritime commerce, prevent or limit the spread of conflict, and prevail in war.

Opportunity and Challenge

The unhindered movement of energy resources, commodities and durable goods by sea is the foundation of the global economic system and of every nation's prosperity to a large extent. This universal dependence on the maritime domain motivates allies and partners alike to collaborate on maintaining maritime security, and to conduct sea control operations as part of a coalition when maritime security is disrupted or insufficient to safeguard global interests.

The challenges to conducting effective sea control operations are diverse and complex; reflective of the diversity of the maritime, space and cyberspace domains that must be concurrently shaped to create the conditions for success, and the complexity of the full-spectrum naval, joint and combined missions that must be planned, resourced and synchronized to realize success. Chief among these challenges are:

■ *Increasingly capable blue water adversaries* that are fielding quiet diesel and nuclear submarines, and new surface combatants armed with advanced torpedoes and anti-ship cruise missiles.

- *Theater anti-access weapons,* including land and anti-ship ballistic missiles (ASBMs), advanced diesel submarines, and associated ISR networks.

- *Area denial weapons in the littoral,* employed by both state and non-state actors, to include mines, coastal defense cruise missiles, swarming fast attack craft, mini-submarines and increasingly quiet and more capable submarines.

- *Technologies that disrupt space and cyberspace capabilities,* particularly command, control, communication, computer, and intelligence (C4I) systems.

Central Idea

Our ability to establish local sea control is fundamental to exploiting the maritime domain as maneuver space, protecting critical sea lines of communication, and projecting and sustaining combat power overseas. The persistent forward presence of U.S. naval forces promotes familiarity with the choke points, sea lanes, and littorals that comprise the strategic maritime geography, as well as the activities and conditions that affect the operational environment. Forward presence also facilitates engagement with allies and partners—many of whom possess potent sea control and power projection capabilities—who may share their superior regional knowledge and contribute to combined sea control operations. Naval forces achieve sea control by neutralizing or destroying threats in the maritime, space and cyberspace domains that constrain our freedom to maneuver, conduct follow-on missions, or restore maritime security.

Achieving Sea Control

Naval forces conduct sea control operations in environments ranging from uncertain to openly hostile, and must frequently contend with adversary tactics such as:

- *Opposed Transit.* An adversary seeks to deny U.S. and allied ability to use the sea lines of communication outside the theater of operations.

- *Anti-access*. An adversary seeks to prevent or delay U.S. and allied ability to approach and access the theater of operations, especially littoral areas, from the open ocean.

- *Area denial*. An adversary seeks to degrade or deny U.S. and allied operational effectiveness or freedom of action within the theater of operations by denying U.S. ability to conduct operations within and across domains, or U.S. ability to project power ashore.

Addressing such threats requires offensive and defensive actions, including the employment of routine protective measures; the episodic countering of imminent attacks; and actively locating and neutralizing, or destroying, adversary threats that are holding naval forces at risk. Beyond traditional kinetic and non-kinetic threats, adversaries will likely conduct space and cyberspace attacks aimed at negating U.S. ability to command and control forces. To the extent possible, naval forces will deploy and employ redundant systems to maintain command and control of dispersed forces in the face of such threats, and will maintain proficiency in retaining the operational and tactical initiative when communications and information systems are degraded or denied. This imperative mandates detailed pre-operational planning and the delegation of authority to leaders with the experience and decision-making skills to exercise independent initiative consistent with commanders' intent.

Opposed Transit

Adversaries with blue water capabilities may threaten combat and support forces transiting from their forward station, forward presence operating area, or point of departure in the continental United States to the theater of operations. Although U.S. naval forces can be surprised while transiting in blue water, there are few threats in the current security environment that can effectively challenge U.S. combatants in the open ocean. Thus, it is likely adversaries will focus on interdicting military sealift, expeditionary strike force, and merchant vessels deploying and sustaining the joint force. Alternatively, or concurrently, adversaries may elect to interdict commercial shipping to degrade the U.S. economy and capacity to support the conflict. In either case, naval forces will be required to neutralize or destroy air, surface and subsurface threats to high value vessels during their transit; using standard escort, area defense, integrated air missile defense, anti-surface warfare and anti-submarine warfare (ASW) tactics, techniques and procedures. The requirement to defend long sea lines of communication can rapidly exceed the capacity of the Naval Service, leading to the use of convoys, routes defended by land-based capabilities, or undefended minimum risk routes. Employing ally and partner naval forces in combined operations to safeguard the deployment of coalition forces can often leverage their knowledge of local conditions, their operational expertise and support from peacetime bases to good effect.

Anti-Access

The range, precision and lethality of anti-ship cruise missiles, ballistic missiles, and diesel submarines are being continuously improved. These capabilities can hold naval forces that are hundreds of miles from an adversary's coast at risk; thereby degrading the U.S. ability to deter potential adversaries, assure allies, and accomplish military objectives with minimal losses. While the Naval Service is engaged in a variety of international initiatives to prevent the proliferation of these anti-access capabilities, it is aggressively enhancing legacy capabilities and developing new ones to disrupt the employment of these evolving threats and to successfully defend against them. Naval forces possess the capability and capacity to mitigate the risks posed by these threats to an acceptable level today, and will be able to deliver the operational and tactical effects expected by the combatant commanders for the foreseeable future. To this end, full spectrum operations in the maritime, space and cyberspace domains will be conducted by naval forces that persist in, neutralize or episodically enter the anti-access environment, depending on mission objectives.

Area Denial

Once naval forces defeat or circumvent opposed transit and anti-access threats to enter an overseas littoral, they become increasingly exposed to an array of land-based air, naval, and ground weapons that can be extended seaward to degrade naval force operational effectiveness. Area-denial weapons include submarines, mini-submarines, fast attack craft, coastal defense cruise missiles, guided munitions and mines. They can be employed by an adversary's conventional forces, special operations forces, or proxy forces; as well as by non-state actors engaged in irregular warfare who may possess them. Area-denial weapons are intended to prevent unconstrained maneuver by U.S. naval forces. Submarines and mini-submarines, tasked with attriting naval forces within a defined operating area, are susceptible to the broad area and tactical ASW systems available to U.S. naval forces. The employment of persistent ISR systems to cue time-sensitive targeting of fast attack craft, coastal defense cruise missiles and guided munitions systems that execute shoot and hide tactics is an effective way to suppress and eventually eliminate these threats. The greatest area-denial challenge in the maritime domain remains mines. Mines are cheap, numerous, widely proliferated, and capable of constraining maneuverability from deep water past the surf zone to the maximum extent of the littoral. Current systems and procedures to clear mines from the deep water through the surf zone are effective, but slow, and in most cases require naval forces to enter the minefield. Moreover, those forces are often subject to harassment by area-denial weapons and fires from the shore. In the future, emerging mine countermeasure capabilities will allow naval forces to more effectively identify and neutralize mines without entering the mine danger area.

Combined Arms Approach to Sea Control

The Naval Service employs a combined-arms approach to achieve sea control. Mission-tailored forces integrate sea, air, land, space, cyberspace, and information operation capabilities employed from ships and submarines; carrier-, amphibious ship- and land-based aircraft; ground vehicles; and remote sites outside the theater of operations; to achieved assigned objectives. Marine amphibious forces, Navy Expeditionary Combat Command forces and the Coast Guard Deployable Operations Group operate cooperatively to bridge the seams between blue, green and brown water, the littoral, and regions further inland. Fleet Cyber Command, Marine Forces Cyberspace Command and Coast Guard Cyber Command conduct full spectrum computer operations in support of every element of the combined-arms team, as well as the joint, interagency and coalition elements that regularly augment naval force packages. The combined-arms approach leverages the following capability advantages to achieve sea control:

- **Superior warfare systems,** which provide robust integrated air and missile defense, including ballistic missile defense; effective undersea warfare; and flexible network-centric attack options using organic and off-board weapons.

- **Large numbers of combat ready platforms,** achieved through enhanced reliability and efficiencies in the inter-deployment training cycle.

- **Increased operational range and endurance**, achieved through improved energy management; increased energy efficiency; and the ability to use a variety of energy sources ranging from nuclear power to conventional petroleum-based fuels and new bio-fuels.

- **Improved interoperability** between U.S. naval forces, other joint forces, allies and partners, achieved through improved networking, new employment concepts that leverage each Service's or partner's strengths and mutually beneficial engagement enabled by persistent forward presence.

- **Resilient communication, navigation, ISR and targeting systems,** redundant pathways for key functions, and preplanned response procedures that ensure naval forces can continue to operate unimpeded by degradations in U.S. satellites or computer networks.

  - **Space Superiority,** which enables dispersed, networked sea control operations through space-based command and control (C2), navigation, targeting, communications, and ISR systems.
  - **Cyberspace Superiority**, enhanced by sound information assurance practices, which ensures that critical networks are defended and full spectrum computer network operations effectively support widely dispersed naval forces engaged in sea control operations.

Summary

Sea control is the foundation of seapower. The ability of U.S. naval forces to establish local and regional sea control is fundamental to exploiting the maritime domain as maneuver space, protecting critical sea lines of communication, and projecting and sustaining combat power overseas. Naval forces achieve sea control by neutralizing or destroying threats in the maritime, space and cyberspace domains that constrain our freedom to maneuver, conduct follow-on missions, or restore maritime security. To this end, naval forces employ a combined-arms approach that leverages the full spectrum of capabilities possessed by the Naval Service, joint force, interagency, allies and partners.

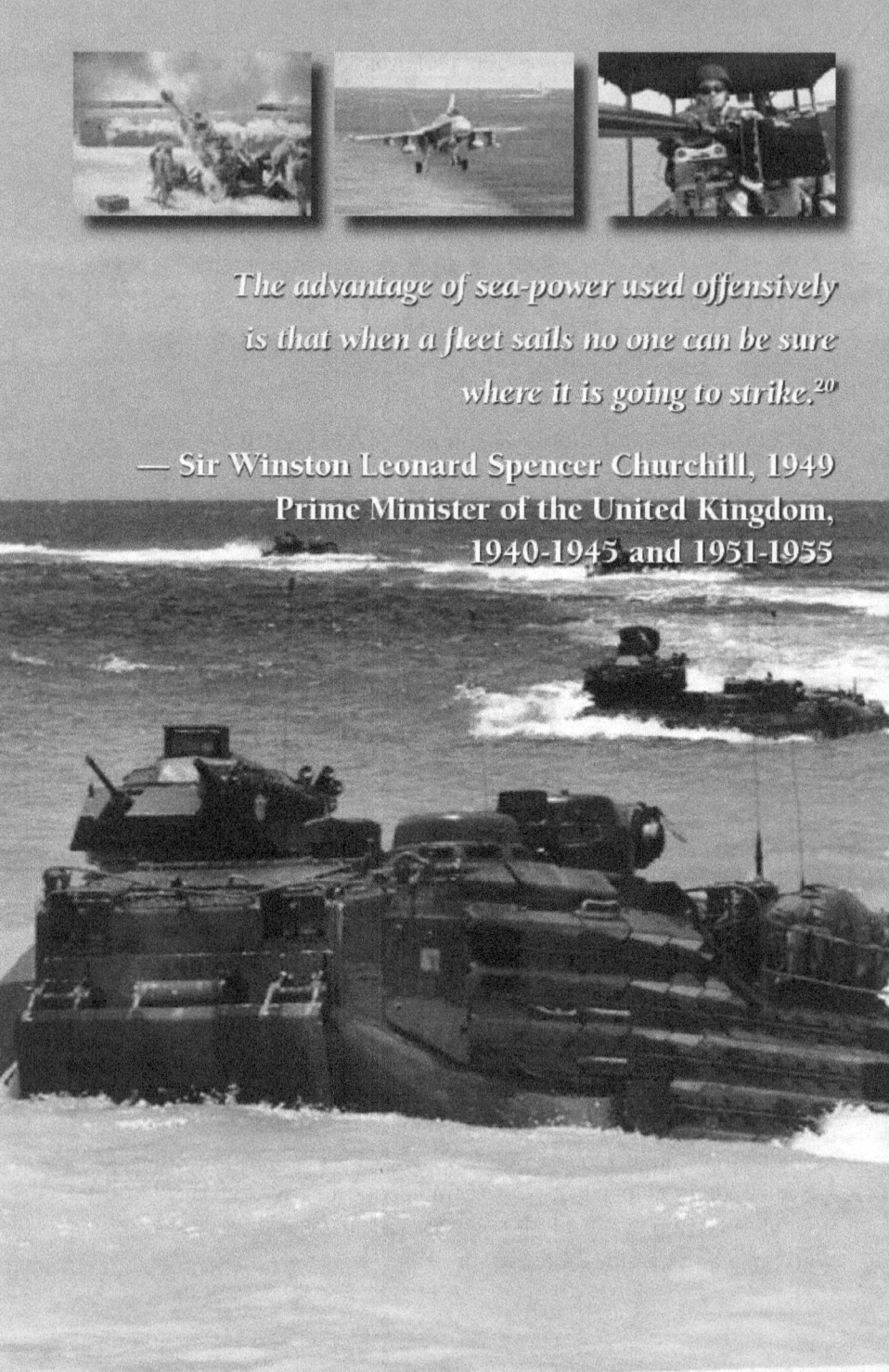

The advantage of sea-power used offensively is that when a fleet sails no one can be sure where it is going to strike.[20]

— Sir Winston Leonard Spencer Churchill, 1949
Prime Minister of the United Kingdom,
1940-1945 and 1951-1955

Chapter 8
Power Projection

*Amphibious flexibility is the greatest strategic asset that a
sea-based power possesses.*[21]

—B.H. Liddell Hart, 1960
Soldier, Military Historian and Theorist

Background

During the Cold War, the United States maintained significant military
forces overseas in close proximity to likely employment areas. Since the
end of that conflict, the United States' global network of air and land
bases has diminished and U.S. military forces have largely transitioned
to an expeditionary posture. Most Naval Service forces are now based
in the United States and deploy overseas, rotationally or episodically, to
meet operational requirements. In this "expeditionary era," U.S. joint
forces are increasingly challenged by geographic, diplomatic, and military
impediments to access, necessitating a greater emphasis on sea-based
power projection capabilities. The *Capstone Concept for Joint Operations*
(CCJO) elaborates on this topic:

> *Diminishing overseas access is another challenge anticipated in the
> future operating environment. Foreign sensitivities to U.S. military
> presence have steadily been increasing. Even close allies may be
> hesitant to grant access for a variety of reasons. Diminished access
> will complicate the maintenance of forward presence, a critical
> aspect of past and current U.S. military strategy, necessitating new
> approaches to responding quickly to developments around the world as
> well as more robust exploitation of existing U.S. advantages to operate
> at sea and in the air, space, and cyberspace. Assuring access to ports,
> airfields, foreign airspace, coastal waters and host nation support
> in potential commitment areas will be a challenge and will require
> active peacetime engagement with states in volatile areas. In war, this
> challenge may require forcible-entry capabilities designed to seize and
> maintain lodgments in the face of armed resistance.*[22]

Power projection in its broadest sense is "the ability of a nation to apply all or some of its elements of national power—political, economic, informational, or military—to rapidly and effectively deploy and sustain forces in and from multiple dispersed locations to respond to crises, to contribute to deterrence, and to enhance regional stability." The United States has two broad *military* means—normally employed in combination—for projecting power overseas: air power and seapower. The Naval Service possesses the capabilities to employ both, in concert with the other elements of national power. Air power provides a means to deliver fires, personnel (to include airborne and air mobile forces), and limited materiel very quickly. It is less effective, however, in delivering equipment and supplies in the volume necessary to sustain larger military operations. Seapower provides a means to deliver fires, personnel (to include amphibious forces), and resources with somewhat less immediacy than air power, but in much greater weight and volume. The preponderance of naval and joint force materiel required to conduct sustained power projection operations is therefore delivered by sea.

Beyond the deployment phase of an operation, strikes and amphibious assaults are the most common naval contributions to power projection. A **strike** is an attack to damage or destroy an objective or capability. Naval strike capabilities include ballistic or cruise missiles, aircraft, naval surface fires, electronic warfare, computer network attack, Marines, and naval special warfare teams.

Operating from international waters, carriers and their embarked air wings are capable of dominating key aspects of the maritime domain for hundreds of miles. The surface combatants and submarines in a carrier strike group (CSG) conduct land attack missile strikes and protect the power projection forces from surface, subsurface, and air threats, including ballistic missiles. The mobility, operational independence, speed, endurance, range and volume of fires provided by a CSG support a wide variety of strike operations. This versatility and lethality is applied across the full range of military operations, from providing sustained, massed fires to defeat enemy ground formations to destroying terrorist base camps; conducting time-sensitive precision strikes against fleeting, high-value targets; protecting friendly forces involved in stability operations; and neutralizing enemy anti-access/area-denial defenses in support of amphibious operations.

An *amphibious assault* involves establishing a landing force on a hostile or potentially hostile shore. Although landing forces may vary in size, they are normally organized as a Marine air-ground task force (MAGTF), each composed of four core elements: a *command element*, a *ground combat element*, an *aviation combat element*, and a *logistics combat element*. The largest, the Marine expeditionary force (MEF), is the Marine Corps' principal warfighting organization and includes at least a Marine division, a Marine aircraft wing, and a Marine logistics group. The Marine expeditionary brigade (MEB) is the "middleweight" MAGTF and is composed of at least one reinforced infantry regiment, a Marine aircraft group, and a combat logistics regiment. The Marine expeditionary unit (MEU) is the typical, forward deployed MAGTF and is composed of a reinforced infantry battalion, a composite squadron of rotary, tilt rotor, and fixed-wing aircraft, and a task-organized logistics combat element. A special purpose MAGTF is a non-standing organization temporarily formed to conduct a specific mission. Amphibious assault ships, amphibious transport dock ships, and dock landing ships provide the afloat staging base required to project, sustain, and recover landing forces, while Navy assault craft units and beachmasters perform key support functions. Additionally, a host of naval capabilities required to establish sea control and neutralize anti-access/area denial threats may be critical to support the conduct of successful amphibious assaults. Additionally, the enhanced maritime prepositioning squadrons provide the means to rapidly reinforce and sustain expeditionary power projection with or without significant port and airfield infrastructure.

While *assault* has been, and remains, the primary impetus for amphibious capabilities, their utility in conducting **raids**, **demonstrations**, **withdrawals**, and **amphibious support to other operations** is immense. U.S. naval forces have conducted more than 107 amphibious operations since 1990, with 78 of them falling into this "other" category. The majority of these were non-combatant evacuations, disaster relief, or similar crisis response operations conducted in austere and uncertain environments. [23] Indeed, one of the largest and most complex amphibious operations in modern history, the withdrawal of more than 6,200 United Nations' peacekeepers from Somalia, was conducted under the threat of surface-to-air missiles in the hands of local militants.

To support large operations, globally dispersed, mission-tailored naval forces rapidly aggregate to form *expeditionary strike forces* (ESFs) capable of projecting overwhelming combat power from the sea. During Operation ENDURING FREEDOM I, for example, an ESF was formed from four carrier battle groups and two amphibious ready groups with embarked Marine expeditionary units (ARG/MEUs). The USS CARL VINSON, THEODORE ROOSEVELT, JOHN C. STENNIS, and ENTER-PRISE provided the preponderance of strike sorties for the operation while the combatants in the ESF employed precision-guided cruise missiles and conducted supporting maritime interdiction operations. The USS PELELIU ARG/15th MEU and USS BATAAN ARG/26th MEU, as Task Force 58, were the first conventional forces ashore in Afghanistan. Projected, supported, and sustained from the North Arabian Sea at a distance of 450 miles, they opened a lodgment for the introduction of additional joint forces. This lodgment, Forward Operating Base Rhino, supported the seizure of Kandahar and subsequent operations several hundred miles further inland.

Opportunity and Challenge

Globally distributed, mission tailored naval forces routinely engage with allies and partners to improve interoperability and to enhance proficiency in the conduct of combined operations. While the vast majority of crisis response operations undertaken by coalitions in recent years have involved sanctions enforcement, stability, humanitarian assistance, disaster relief and maritime interdiction missions, the experience gained is valuable when circumstances require naval forces to mount a major power projection campaign—as occurred with Operation ENDURING FREEDOM. The persistent forward presence of U.S. naval forces not only enables such engagement and combined crisis response operations; it also facilitates the initiatives of the other elements of national power to inspire like-minded nations to project power together for the common good.

While the Naval Service is capable of overcoming the geographic challenges inherent in projecting power globally, and enjoys fewer impediments to access than the other Services, naval forces face increasingly capable anti-access and area-denial threats. This circumstance requires naval and supporting forces to shape conditions synchronously across the sea, undersea, air, land, space and cyberspace domains in order to achieve assigned power projection objectives within acceptable risk. Additionally, the advantages in naval force capability and capacity enjoyed by many allies and partners with whom we have habitually shared common national security interests—and indeed those of the United States—relative to potential adversaries are declining over time. Coupled with an increasing number of diverse, concurrent crises perpetrated by both state and non-state actors, these circumstances demand that the Naval Service creatively apply its inherent adaptability, flexibility and reach to project power effectively.

Central Idea

The character of a power projection operation reflects the objective—such as destroying an adversary's invading ground force or securing and restoring a partner's commercial port capacity; and the operating environment—permissive, uncertain or hostile. In combination, these factors drive base, branch and sequel planning; tactics, techniques and procedures to be employed; and the tailored naval forces to be committed.

A *permissive environment* is one in which the host country military and law enforcement agencies are able to maintain control of the operating area, and have the capability and intent to assist the operation. Forward postured naval forces routinely conduct a broad spectrum of power projection missions in permissive environments. The capabilities that allow naval forces to project and sustain combat power against a hostile adversary are the same capabilities that allow them to overcome damaged or limited local infrastructure; extract personnel from hazardous circumstances; provide emergency care; and restore the critical enablers for health and safety. Mobile command and control (C2), well decks, flight decks, surface and air connectors, emergency medical capability and cargo capacity all allow *globally distributed, mission-tailored* naval forces to conduct sea-based evacuations; respond to disasters; and when necessary, facilitate the introduction of additional naval, joint, interagency, multinational and non-governmental capabilities as part of a "whole of government" or international response.

An *uncertain environment* is one in which the host government forces, whether opposed to or supportive of the operation, lack effective control of the territory and population in the operating area. Forward postured naval forces frequently conduct noncombatant evacuation and embassy reinforcement missions in uncertain environments. Increasingly, naval forces are being tasked to project power into ungoverned or under-governed areas being exploited as safe havens by terrorists, weapons traffickers, pirates, and other criminal elements. Counterterrorism, counter-piracy and counter-proliferation missions can involve strikes and amphibious raids conducted to kill or capture terrorists; destroy insurgent training camps; capture pirates or other criminals; seize illegal arms and contraband; rescue hostages; and secure, safeguard or remove weapons of mass destruction (WMD). Stability operations—such as those ongoing in Afghanistan, and the 1995 amphibious withdrawal of United Nations' peacekeeping forces from Somalia—are representative of large scale power projection operations conducted in an uncertain environment.

Operations in an uncertain environment are always conducted with the expectation of armed opposition. While potential adversaries—including non-state actors—are unlikely to mount fully integrated anti-access defense in an uncertain environment, they often possess a variety of lethal area denial weapons. Naval forces limit the effectiveness of such weapons through evolutionary tactics and new technologies that enhance over-the-horizon operations; connector range, speed and agility; shipboard defenses; mine and improvised explosive device (IED) coun-termeasures, and counter-fire, especially for the immediate suppression of threats. Information operations, to include deception, psychological operations, and the non-kinetic neutralization of adversaries' C2 systems, are also employed in lieu of or in addition to kinetic attacks depending on the mission objective and extant rules of engagement.

A **hostile environment** is one in which adversary forces have control of the operating area, as well as the capability and intent to oppose the operation. The most challenging power projection mission in a hostile environment is an amphibious assault to enable the introduction and sustainment of a large follow-on force. Such operations require the full spectrum of naval, joint, and interagency capabilities to successfully establish local sea control and project power ashore. To this end, naval forces must accomplish three major, overlapping tasks.

Gaining and Maintaining Operational Access

Gaining and maintaining operational access in a sophisticated hostile environment will invariably require the full spectrum of lethal, non-lethal, conventional and special capabilities possessed by the United States, applied synchronously to shape and achieve advantage in the sea, undersea, air, land, space and cyberspace domains. The establishment of sea control, discussed at length in the previous chapter, permits the use of the sea as maneuver space and is an essential pre-condition for the use of **strike operations** to conduct decisive power projection ashore. When naval forces possess sufficient capabilities to **persist** in the operating area and successfully accomplish their assigned tasks while concurrently defending against the anti-access threats, sea control can be achieved and conditions can be set to project power ashore rapidly. As the reach, diversity, density and sophistication of anti-access capabilities increase, naval forces may establish local, **episodic** sea control in support of raids and other short duration amphibious operations if such a scheme of maneuver is sufficient to accomplish the operational objectives. Otherwise, naval forces will use power projection operations—largely from the CSGs, their surface combatant escorts, and supporting submarines—to **systematically neutralize** robust anti-access threats in advance of the maneuver force.

Conducting Littoral Maneuver

Littoral maneuver is the ability to transition ready-to-fight combat forces from the sea to the shore in order to achieve a position of advantage over the enemy. It may be employed directly against an objective, including inland objectives, to accomplish the mission singly; to seize infrastructure or lodgments that will enable the arrival of follow-on forces; or to pose a continuous coastal threat that causes an adversary to fix, maneuver or dissipate his forces.

The naval force capabilities employed to achieve sea control remain critical during littoral maneuver. Advanced, networked space-based sensors; long-range, persistent unmanned aircraft; and locally deployable air, surface and subsurface multi-spectral intelligence, surveillance, and reconnaissance (ISR) systems provide naval forces with improved battlefield awareness, rapid target acquisition/designation, and superior all-weather/obscured visibility combat effectiveness. Carrier air wings and sea-based Marine tactical aviation provide air superiority over the amphibious operations area, air interdiction of adversary forces maneuvering toward the landing force, and close air support to augment high-volume naval surface fires from surface combatants. Rotary-wing aircraft, armed with air-to-surface missiles, embarked on surface combatants and amphibious assault ships, along with vertical/short takeoff and landing fixed wing aircraft from amphibious assault ships contribute fires in the littoral as required. Moreover, non-kinetic fires provided by electronic warfare systems and computer network operations can be employed to gain the initiative.

The mission, geography, weather and adversary's capabilities all combine to create a unique set of seaward and landward littoral maneuver challenges. Adversary aircraft, coastal defenses, air defenses, submarines, surface combatants, fast attack craft (including suicide boats), maneuver forces, improvised explosive devices and mines (in the sea and very shallow water as well as on land), and a collection of weapons often referred to as G-RAMM—guided rockets, artillery, mortars and missiles—must all be effectively countered. Additionally, littoral maneuver may also be subject to attack by irregular forces employing a variety of simple and sophisticated weapons.

To offset these threats, especially widely proliferated first-generation anti-ship cruise missiles (ASCMs), assault echelons will normally commence littoral maneuver from amphibious ships positioned—at least initially—over-the-horizon. This extends the range from, and reduces the ISR available to, the adversary. MEBs will normally provide the landing force building blocks for larger contingencies and major operations. When combined, two MEB assault echelons constitute the assault echelon of a MEF. Naval forces use high-speed vertical and surface means, singularly or in combination depending on the threat environment, to rapidly project this combat power ashore. During Operation DESERT STORM in 1991, for example, an all-vertical assault into the Al Wafrah gap was conducted due to the high concentration of sea mines. During Operation UNITED SHIELD in 1995, the amphibious withdrawal of United Nations forces from Somalia employed surface means only in order to avoid a significant surface-to-air missile threat.

Enhanced MAGTF operations incorporate landing force capability and capacity refinements that improve the self-sufficiency of smaller units so that they can operate over greater ranges and for extended duration, as well as increasing their ability to operate from a wider variety of ships. It also includes the ability to conduct larger-scale operations by transitioning numerous maneuver units ashore via multiple, distributed points—versus establishing a single, contiguous beachhead—in order to avoid established defenses, natural obstacles, and the presentation of a concentrated, lucrative target.

By keeping its command, aviation, and logistics elements afloat to the maximum extent possible, the MAGTF will further reduce vulnerabilities ashore while retaining a high degree of mobility and dexterity. This approach provides multiple options for employment of the ground combat element within the joint or multinational force commander's scheme of maneuver. Included among those options is the ability to re-embark the ground combat element to conduct further amphibious operations aimed at outflanking an adversary, cutting enemy supply lines, or simply outpacing overland movement.

Sustained littoral operations may also include the employment of coastal and riverine forces. Depending upon the environment and the mission, these forces may operate as independent units or be task-organized in combination with amphibious and strike forces. Embarkation of Marines, Coast Guardsmen, or Navy Maritime Expeditionary Security Force personnel aboard littoral combatants provides additional force employment options.

Enabling the Arrival of Joint or Multinational Forces
Naval forces may be tasked with enabling the rapid build-up of joint or multinational forces in the objective area. Inasmuch as the finite number of amphibious ships will be committed to the assault echelons conducting littoral maneuver, the arrival of follow-on forces will be accomplished primarily through **naval movement.** Naval movement involves military sealift and merchant vessels transporting vehicles, equipment, and supplies in volume over strategic distances for offload at a port or expeditionary facility. Naval movement is normally employed in concert with the movement of personnel by strategic airlift.

Maritime prepositioning forces, which are composed of one or more maritime prepositioning ship squadrons loaded with follow-on force materiel; a Navy support element; and a MAGTF fly-in echelon, exemplify the combination of naval movement and strategic airlift. Maritime prepositioning forces play a crucial role in rapidly reinforcing the assault echelons and bringing the full capabilities of the MEF into action. This approach merges the weight and volume advantages of sealift with the speed of airlift. However, unlike littoral maneuver, which projects units in a ready-to-fight condition, naval movement and strategic airlift are dependent upon secure infrastructure ashore to accept disaggregated elements, which must go through the process of reception, staging, onward movement, and integration before units can be employed. Naval movement and strategic airlift must therefore be enabled by seizing existing infrastructure intact or securing a lodgment for the establishment of expeditionary facilities.

The seizure of existing ports and airfields intact is not always possible. Adversaries often concentrate defensive capabilities around these facilities and destroy key infrastructure when seizure becomes imminent. Even successful seizures can cause combat damage, and in some cases key infrastructure may not exist. Naval forces must therefore be capable of mine countermeasures operations, explosive ordnance disposal, and construction engineering in order to rapidly repair existing facilities or build expeditionary facilities. Sometimes, the joint force commander may intentionally avoid established ports and airfields—at least initially—in order to make his scheme of maneuver less predictable. Current high-speed intra-theater connectors are capable of offloading onto austere facilities in a secure area, and expeditionary causeway systems can reduce reliance on existing infrastructure. In all cases, naval cargo handlers, combat logisticians, and maritime security forces facilitate the introduction of follow-on forces and other resources.

The dependence upon secure infrastructure ashore is being partially alleviated through enhancements to maritime prepositioning and other forms of military sealift. Providing the ability to conduct selective offload and at-sea transfer of personnel and equipment from sealift platforms to amphibious ships or directly to air and surface craft capable of ship-to-shore delivery will enable a more sea-based approach.[24]

Naval Expeditionary Logistics

The ability to sustain naval forces—whether globally dispersed or aggregated to project power—is accomplished through an extensive defense distribution system comprised of military bases at home and abroad; expeditionary enabling and support forces; joint capabilities; host and partner nations; and private vendors. Built around the combat logistics force ships and support ships operated by the Military Sealift Command, naval expeditionary logistics provide an end-to-end supply chain capable of continuously providing parts, supplies, and equipment from the continental United States, or intermediate advanced bases, directly to naval forces at sea. With these assets, the full range of logistics distribution functions are possible even when overseas shore-based support is limited or nonexistent. The ability to conduct logistics functions afloat enables naval forces to maintain station anywhere. The Navy and Marine Corps are moving beyond logistics interoperability to Naval Logistics Integration (NLI), which is enhancing the Naval Service's ability to provide sea-based support to naval as well as joint and multinational forces operating at sea or ashore.

Command and Control Enhancements

The complexity, tempo, and distributed nature of power projection operations require precise coordination among all elements of the force, fully interoperable ISR sensors, processing systems, and associated data transport systems; and the ability to collect, process, and disseminate relevant information in near real time to support distributed fires and maneuver. These operational capabilities are being incorporated into Navy maritime operations center (MOC) and Marine Corps C2 capabilities, afloat and ashore. Additional C2 enhancements are simultaneously increasing protection of network, intelligence, and decision aid architectures that support decentralized execution and enhance joint coordination. Concurrently, collaborative planning, rehearsal, execution and assessment tools are being proliferated and beyond-line-of-sight, over-the-horizon, and on-the-move systems capable of operating in a degraded communications environment are being considered for landing forces and support craft. In many operating environments, however, this level of connectivity may be difficult to sustain, as emerging anti-satellite weapons, jamming technologies and precision strike weapons may damage or degrade U.S. network infrastructure. To allow effective power projection in the face of these challenges, the Naval Service has developed procedures to operate with only line-of-sight or no communications and is reducing its reliance on reach-back support, while at the same time establishing more resilient networks that rely on distributed and redundant nodes in space, the atmosphere and on the surface.

Summary

Globally distributed, mission-tailored naval forces and *regionally concentrated naval forces* both routinely project power. The character of a power projection operation reflects the mission and the operating environment—permissive, uncertain or hostile. Gaining and maintaining operational access in a sophisticated hostile environment will invariably require the full spectrum of lethal, non-lethal, conventional and special capabilities possessed by the United States, applied synchronously to shape and achieve advantage in the sea, undersea, air, land, space and cyberspace domains. ***Strike operations***, executed primarily by the nuclear-powered aircraft carriers' (CVNs') embarked air wings, and surface and sub-surface launched land attack missiles, are our principal means of gaining and maintaining operational access.

The establishment of sea control permits the use of the sea as maneuver space and is an essential pre-condition for decisive power projection ashore. ***Littoral maneuver*** is the ability to transition ready-to-fight combat forces from the sea to the shore in order to achieve a position of advantage over the enemy. It may be employed directly against an objective, including inland objectives, to accomplish the mission singly; to seize infrastructure or lodgments that will enable the arrival of follow-on forces; or to pose a continuous coastal threat that causes an adversary to fix, maneuver or dissipate his forces. The naval force capabilities employed to achieve sea control remain critical during littoral maneuver.

MEBs will normally provide the landing force building blocks for larger contingencies and major operations. When combined, two MEB assault echelons constitute the assault echelon of a MEF. Naval forces use high-speed vertical and surface means, singularly or in combination depending on the threat environment, to rapidly project this combat power ashore. ***Enhanced MAGTF operations*** incorporate landing force capability and capacity refinements that improve the self-sufficiency of smaller units so that they can operate over greater ranges and for extended duration, as well as increasing their ability to assault from a wider variety of ships.

71

Lying offshore, ready to act, the presence of ships and
Marines sometimes means much more than just
having air power or ship's fire, when it comes to
deterring a crisis. And the ships and Marines may
not have to do anything but lie offshore. It is hard to lie
offshore with a C-141 or C-130 full of airborne troops.

— General Colin Powell, U.S. Army, 1990
65th Secretary of State and 12th Chairman
of the Joint Chiefs of Staff

Chapter 9
Deterrence

Indeed, force is never more operative than when it is known to exist but is not brandished.[25]

—Alfred Thayer Mahan, 1912
Naval Historian and Theorist

Background

Naval forces have historically provided nuclear and conventional means to discourage aggression and dissuade adversaries from hostile action. The ability of naval forces to rapidly deploy and indefinitely sustain credible combat power worldwide provides national decision-makers with an important tool to signal U.S. intent and resolve, deterring adversaries, assuring allies, and contributing to homeland defense in depth.[26]

The Maritime Strategy underscores that preventing wars is preferable to fighting wars. This emphasis on war prevention calls for an expanded concept of deterrence to meet 21st-century threats.

Collectively, *forward presence, maritime security, humanitarian assistance and disaster response (HA/DR), sea control,* and *power projection* support and sustain an expanded form of *deterrence.* Going further, *A Cooperative Strategy for 21st Century Seapower* (CS-21) provided the Naval Service with a purposefully expanded view of deterrence. This new framework includes conducting prevention activities intended to address the conditions that lead to conflict, while discouraging aggressors through cooperative action and partnership.

Opportunity and Challenge

In the 21st century the United States faces an expanding array of adversaries who threaten its vital interests. This includes both state and non-state actors who may pose regional, transnational, or global threats through irregular, conventional or nuclear means. Some potential adversaries may not be deterred with nuclear or conventional retaliation, and may actually seek to elicit a U.S. reprisal to support their own strategic objectives. As described in previous chapters, U.S. forces are required to conduct a variety of military tasks, equally capable of *globally distributed* or *regionally concentrated* projection of both "hard power" and "soft power" as appropriate. This presents a challenge for naval forces—maintaining their advantages to prevent and deter conflict through nuclear and conventional means while evolving new, non-traditional deterrence capabilities.

Central Idea

Effective deterrence requires a comprehensive effort that includes all elements of national power. In support of this expanded approach, the Naval Service will employ a broader set of capabilities to assure partners, dissuade adversaries, and deter or limit hostile action. These include continued nuclear and conventional combat preeminence, as well as new capabilities to deter evolving threats posed by an array of current and potential adversaries.

CS-21 calls for the naval forces to build confidence and trust among nations through collective security efforts that focus on common threats and mutual interests with an unprecedented level of cooperation within the Naval Service and the other instruments of national power and U.S. international partners. In this environment, deterrent effects are achieved through the inherent combat power of forward postured naval task forces, as well as *globally distributed mission-tailored forces* engaged in fostering, expanding and strengthening cooperative relationships, promoting stable and prosperous regional conditions, and preventing crises.

An Expanded Deterrence Framework

Deployed naval forces are uniquely suited to this *expanded approach to deterrence*. They possess a credible and scalable ability to deter state and non-state adversaries using nuclear and conventional means. Through their inherent ability to maneuver, largely unfettered by diplomatic challenges to access and presence, naval forces support a wide range of credible deterrence options. To sustain this core capability, naval forces must continue to develop a broad and enduring deterrence portfolio by maintaining nuclear and conventional capability advantages, including sea-based ballistic missile defense (BMD).

In addition, globally distributed naval forces—postured forward and in coordination with U.S. Government and international sea service partners—generate an expanded and non-traditional set of preventative deterrent effects through partnerships, cooperative security and engagement. These prevention activities, focused on addressing regional, transnational, and global security challenges, are designed to limit the influence and constrain the actions of rogue governments and non-state actors.

Collectively, this cumulative and mutually supporting framework provides U.S. national leadership with expanded deterrence options across a range of security challenges, and is the expanded deterrence capability the Nation requires.

Nuclear Deterrence

The backbone of the Nation's survivable nuclear deterrent will continue to be provided by the ballistic missile submarine (SSBN) force and its supporting command and control (C2) architecture. This demonstrated capability provides an enduring and credible deterrent against any state that would threaten, or actually employ, nuclear weapons.

SSBNs serve as the ultimate guarantor of the U.S. assured second-strike capability. They are designed specifically for stealth and the precision delivery of nuclear warheads. As a virtually undetectable and survivable launch platform, SSBNs ensure that the United States will have sufficient nuclear forces to inflict unacceptable consequences on an adversary in response to a nuclear attack.

.

We will continue to provide a nuclear deterrent that is persistent and maintained in a ready posture, while remaining subject to firm C2 procedures and protected from conventional or irregular attack. The credibility and survivability upon which this deterrence rests is dependent upon robust acoustic and non-acoustic stealth, reliable long-range missiles, and an adaptable employment concept capable of holding adversaries at risk anywhere on the globe. To maintain a robust, secure and survivable nuclear deterrent, we will develop the technologies and communications architecture necessary to support the next generation of sea-based strategic deterrence.

Conventional Deterrence

It is difficult to overstate the time-tested conventional deterrent value of a forward postured, sustained and combat-capable naval force. Potential adversaries are constrained in their freedom to act by the probability of retaliation from overwhelming and technologically advanced offensive capabilities, combined with defensive measures that allow naval forces to fight effectively despite growing anti-access and area-denial capabilities.

Conventional deterrence puts a premium on the credible ability to rapidly respond to aggression, and therefore *regionally concentrated, combat-credible* naval power plays a central role. Naval forces can quickly respond to emerging crises by bringing combat power where none existed before, and they can augment existing forces already in theater to signal U.S. political resolve in a crisis and further swing the local balance of power in the United States' favor. The ability to rapidly deploy, and indefinitely sustain, combat power in a region helps ensure that an opponent cannot hope to wait out U.S. forces in the belief that at some point there will be a favorable "window of opportunity" for conventional aggression. Forward presence, sea control and power projection preeminence deter aggression through the credible threat of conventional retaliation and the certain denial of an adversary's military objectives.

A key to denying adversary objectives in the emerging strategic environment are effective **maritime ballistic missile defense** forces. Several nations have developed, tested and fielded ballistic missiles that threaten the U.S homeland, its territories, its forces deployed abroad, and its partners, friends and allies. Emerging technologies will make it possible for potential adversaries to inhibit naval forces from accessing littoral regions through the employment of short and medium-range ballistic missiles designed to attack ships at sea. As ballistic missile technology advances and proliferates, more nations are gaining or will gain the means necessary to attack both sovereign U.S. territory and deployed U.S. forces. The Nation has called for a BMD architecture that includes complementary capabilities for mid-course interception of missiles outside of friendly airspace and point defense protection of population centers, critical infrastructure and military bases. The Navy provides a deployable mid-course interception capability, which is already employed in the Western Pacific, Middle Eastern and European theaters. In addition to these maturing kinetic defense capabilities, we will continue to emphasize non-kinetic and "prior to launch" solutions that defeat the ballistic missile threat.

Today, the robust air and missile defense capability of cruisers and destroyers is leveraged for maritime BMD. With the proper combat system upgrades, they will be able to focus sensors hundreds of miles over land to persistently monitor the airspace above a launch site. If a missile launch is detected, these ships can cue either sea-based or ground-based interceptors with accurate tracking and targeting data, and if equipped with advanced surface-to-air missiles, autonomously intercept incoming missiles.

Surface combatants operating in international waters have great flexibility and can reposition in order to improve detection and interception. Ships conducting sea-based missile defense are sometimes tethered to a nominal station, which could leave them less capable of other missions such as undersea warfare or strike. As a result, single-mission land systems are a more operationally and financially efficient method to address a fixed, known threat than equivalently capable multi-mission surface combatants. As the ballistic missile threat continues to grow across the globe, the Navy's maritime BMD capabilities may be called upon to respond in all theaters. When expanded through the employment of linked maritime operations centers (MOCs), sea- and land-based ballistic missile defenses can be integrated into a globally deployable capability, scalable and responsive to the threat.

Preventive Deterrence through Partnership
Effective theater security cooperation (TSC) and similar "soft power" activities promote a collective approach to mutual defense concerns while also addressing the conditions that result in conflict, thereby generating non-traditional deterrent effects. In this expanded deterrence framework partnership, cooperation and engagement strengthen relationships and extend overall capacities to stabilize and secure the maritime commons, creating effective and enduring disincentives to negative behavior. With maritime safety and security as a foundation for cooperation, global maritime partnerships enhance regional, transnational, and global security while also eroding support for disruptive extremist ideologies. Building partner capacity empowers like-minded maritime nations to address local and regional security issues and deter adversaries; and expands the reach

of the international maritime community to address other threats, such as the proliferation of weapons of mass destruction (WMD). In this manner, the Naval Service's cooperative engagement activities and partner capacity-building enhance the conditions that promote stability, prosperity and good governance within the global maritime commons. This is an approach advocated by the Chairman of the Joint Chiefs of Staff:

> *Give people something positive to hold on to instead of something negative to avoid. Give parents a chance to raise their children to a better standard of living than the one they themselves enjoyed. Do that and we deter not the tactics of terrorists—they will still try to kill—but rather the ends that they seek to achieve.*[27]

Summary

As the Nation evolves its deterrence capabilities to meet the diverse challenges of the global security environment, it is important that naval forces appropriately apply the full range of nuclear, conventional, and cooperative means available to deter actions by state and non-state adversaries that threaten U.S. interests at home or abroad.

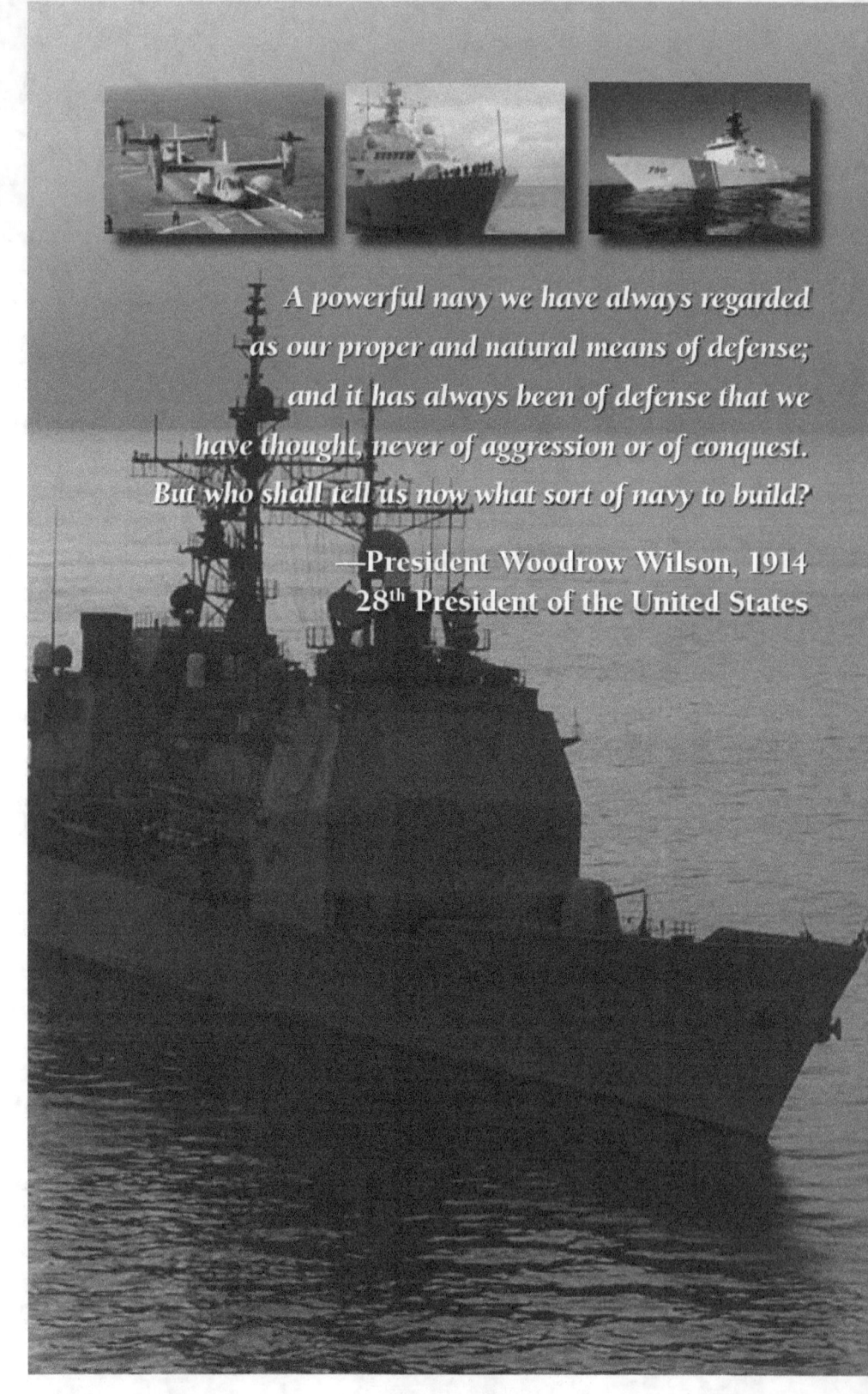

A powerful navy we have always regarded
as our proper and natural means of defense;
and it has always been of defense that we
have thought, never of aggression or of conquest.
But who shall tell us now what sort of navy to build?

—President Woodrow Wilson, 1914
28th President of the United States

Chapter 10
Future Force Structure

So far from being in any way a provocation to war, an adequate and highly trained navy is the best guarantee against war, the cheapest and most effective peace insurance. The cost of building and maintaining such a navy represents the very lightest premium for insuring peace which this nation can possibly pay.... The American people must either build and maintain an adequate navy, or else make up their minds definitely to accept a secondary position in international affairs, not merely in political, but in commercial, matters.

—President Theodore Roosevelt, 1901
26ᵗʰ President of the United States

Background

This *Naval Operations Concept* describes when, where and how U.S. naval forces are employed to prevent conflict and prevail in war. These demands place a premium on recruiting, developing, and retaining high quality Sailors, Marines, and Coast Guardsmen who are capable of adapting to a wide range of operational conditions and missions. To execute the Maritime Strategy and protect U.S. national interests, naval forces must be able to provide *regionally concentrated, credible combat power*, to include establishing sea control and projecting power whenever and wherever required. As the Maritime Strategy emphasizes, however, conducting theater security cooperation (TSC) and building maritime partnerships are equally essential elements of protecting access to the global commons, mitigating the causes of conflict and deterring aggression. These efforts require *globally distributed, mission-tailored forces*. U.S. naval forces must also provide deterrence from nuclear attack against the homeland, and provide regional defense for U.S. forces, infrastructure, allies and partners against theater ballistic missile threats. These efforts require *strategic deterrent forces*.

Opportunity and Challenge

The preceding chapters described how the Naval Service executes its core capabilities in a security environment characterized by an increasing number of concurrent, diverse nuclear, conventional and irregular challenges, perpetrated by both state and non-state actors, that is evolving toward a new multi-polar balance of global power. The United States and particularly the Naval Service recognize the importance of allies and partners in this environment, and are committed to collaboratively building the interoperability and capacity necessary to share the burden of achieving global maritime security and providing for the common defense of like-minded nations. To this end, the Naval Service is rebalancing its force structure to address the blue, green and brown water threats potentially posed by very capable state adversaries, as well as the maritime security and irregular littoral challenges posed by both state and non-state adversaries.

While armed conflicts between states occur infrequently, they are the greatest threat to the United States and demand sufficient numbers of technologically advanced "high-end" capabilities to ensure the United States can effectively deter, dissuade and if necessary defeat a peer competitor. Deterrence is enhanced and risk reduced if the Naval Service, allies and partners—in the aggregate—possess the high-end capability and capacity to *decisively* project power to counter coercion and aggression. Considering the growing costs of technologically advanced capabilities; the demand for balanced "high"- and "low"-end capabilities; and the intense competition for funding across all elements of national power, the Naval Service and its ally and partner counterparts are significantly challenged to sustain the naval forces necessary to project the power required in today's—and tomorrow's—security environment.

Central Idea

Naval Operations Concept 2010 (NOC 10) provides the basis for assessing the forces required to implement *A Cooperative Strategy for 21st Century Seapower* (CS-21). The Naval Service capabilities herein are carefully designed to address the requirement to concurrently enhance global maritime security, prevent and respond to crises, deter aggression, and defeat very capable adversaries. To this end, they have been informed by the operational needs of the combatant commanders and by current and anticipated resource constraints.

Aircraft Carriers

Nuclear-powered aircraft carriers (CVNs) and their embarked air wings provide responsive, flexible, sustainable strike capability and capacity that does not require diplomatic access. Aircraft carriers serve as the centerpiece of carrier strike groups (CSGs) during power projection operations. In the event of conflict, multiple CSGs can aggregate, along with other surge forces if required, to form an expeditionary strike force capable of projecting significant power at-sea and ashore.

The standard CSG force package includes a CVN, air wing, up to five surface combatants, a direct support submarine, and a combat logistics force ship. The ships provide integrated air and missile defense (IAMD) to include ballistic missile defense; and strike warfare, undersea warfare, surface warfare, maritime security, and sustainment. When not conducting coordinated operations, these ships will often disaggregate to conduct dispersed security cooperation, counter-piracy, counter-terrorism or other maritime security operations in the theater.

In meeting steady-state combatant commander demand, the Naval Service will continue to maintain three CVNs forward deployed in regions of critical national interest. In addition to the three deployed CVNs, the inter-deployment training and maintenance process allows a minimum of two additional CVNs to be ready in 30 days and one additional CVN to be ready in 90 days, under a 3-2-1 construct. Adaptive force packaging will adjust the composition of each associated CSG to meet specific mission requirements.

Aircraft

Aircraft provide a unique combination of speed, endurance, agility, reach and firepower, which complement other naval capabilities. Manned and unmanned naval aircraft are fully integrated into the majority of naval operations, performing a wide variety of functions and tasks. These include strike operations; offensive and defensive counter-air operations (OCA/DCA); offensive air support and assault support for landing forces as well as joint or multinational forces ashore; maritime patrol; surveillance and reconnaissance; airborne early warning; surface warfare; undersea warfare; electronic warfare; command and control (C2); logistics support; and search and rescue operations.

Naval aircraft can be described in three broad categories: fixed wing aircraft; rotary-wing/tilt-rotor aircraft; and unmanned aerial systems. Aircraft from all three categories may be task-organized to provide the capability and capacity necessary to perform specific missions. Four common organizational constructs provide the basis for describing the Naval Service aviation force structure.

Carrier air wings are comprised of aircraft designed to operate from CVNs. Each of ten wings embarks on a single carrier and will typically be comprised of four fighter/attack squadrons, one electronic warfare squadron, one early warning and control squadron, one or two helicopter squadrons, a two-plane fleet logistics support detachment and a detachment of unmanned aerial vehicles.

Marine air wings constitute the aviation combat element of each Marine expeditionary force (MEF). They are designed to operate from a combination of ships and austere airfields. Their assets can be task-organized to support deployed Marine expeditionary units (MEUs) as well as Marine expeditionary brigades (MEBs) or special purpose Marine air-ground task forces (SP MAGTFs). Additionally, Marine fighter/attack squadrons are provided on a scheduled rotational basis to selected carrier air wings as part of Tactical Aviation Integration (TAI). Given their different mission portfolio, Marine air wings should not be confused with carrier air wings in size or composition. While the exact structure of each Marine air wing varies slightly, they are generally composed of six or seven fighter/attack squadrons, three vertical/short take-off and landing attack squadrons, one electronic attack squadron, five or six attack helicopter squadrons, six or seven medium lift helicopter or tilt-rotor squadrons, three or four heavy lift helicopter squadrons, a refueling/transport squadron, a squadron of unmanned aerial systems, as well as organic C2 and expeditionary support groups. Marine rotary wing and tilt-rotor aircraft may be task-organized to support distributed operations from amphibious ships or austere locations ashore. In addition to providing the ability to command and control air operations, and operate in an expeditionary environment as a result of the aviation logistics capabilities resident in the Marine wing support squadrons, the Marine air wing also contributes key capabilities that support the MAGTF command element's ability to function as the nucleus of a joint task force headquarters.

Shipboard aviation detachments are designed to operate from ships with smaller flight decks. These usually include two or three helicopters and/or unmanned aerial vehicles conducting sea control missions such as surveillance, undersea warfare, surface warfare, maritime interdiction operations, and mine countermeasures; as well as security cooperation, logistics support, maritime reconnaissance and patrol, law enforcement, and search and rescue tasks. In cases where aircraft cannot embark on a ship, helicopters and tilt-rotor aircraft may use ships with flight decks as refueling "lily-pads" to extend their range or time on mission.

Land-based aviation units operate from U.S., ally and partner facilities, and are critical to our capability to establish sea control and conduct power projection operations. These aviation units include both manned and unmanned systems, and conduct a variety of operations, such as maritime reconnaissance and patrol, electronic warfare, aerial refueling, surface warfare and undersea warfare. Navy, Marine, and Coast Guard land-based aviation units may also be employed to conduct maritime reconnaissance and patrol, search and rescue, aerial refueling, logistics support, law enforcement, and environmental response activities.

Amphibious Ships

The capabilities which allow an amphibious task force to provide globally distributed presence and rapid crisis response are the same capabilities that allow them to overcome limited or damaged local infrastructure during humanitarian assistance and disaster response (HA/DR) missions and when aggregated, assure access through the delivery and support of an amphibious expeditionary landing force on a hostile shore. C2 suites, flight decks, well decks, vertical and surface connectors, medical facilities, and carrying capacity allow amphibious forces to conduct sea-based security cooperation activities; build partnership capacity; respond to natural and manmade disasters; and, when necessary, facilitate the introduction of additional naval, joint, multinational, interagency, international, or non-governmental organization capabilities. As a result, amphibious ships are especially useful in supporting rotational ARG/MEU forward presence, global fleet station and special purpose MAGTF initiatives. In the event of conflict, forward stationed and rotationally deployed amphibious forces can aggregate with surged forces to overcome military access challenges and respond to crises up to major theater war.

Maritime Prepositioning

Prepositioning ships are operated by the Military Sealift Command (MSC)[28] and are forward postured where they can quickly close on areas of vital national interest. Currently three maritime prepositioning ship (MPS) squadrons are employed to carry Marine Corps equipment, supplies and ammunition as well as Seabee, expeditionary airfield, and field hospital equipment and cargo. The composition of the MPS squadrons provides the flexibility to respond to a broad spectrum of crises and support the full range of military operations. These ships have their own cranes, lighterage, and roll-on/roll-off ramps for pier-side offload in a secure port or in-stream in a secure near-shore area. Future enhancements to the prepositioning fleet will improve its ability to support vertical and surface means of arrival, assembly, employment, sustainment and reconstitution of forces at sea.

New concepts for employment of prepositioning ships will increase their relevance and utility in steady state HA/DR, maritime security and maritime security force assistance (MSFA) operations, as well as their enduring role in power projection operations, where little or no port and airfield infrastructure exists and over-the-beach off-load is a necessity. These concepts will modify the loading and operations of prepositioning ships to balance the needs of steady state operations with those of large-scale power projection operations. Each of the three MPS squadrons is being significantly enhanced with a large medium-speed, roll-on/roll-off ship (LMSR), a dry cargo/ammunition ship (T-AKE) and a mobile landing platform (MLP). In addition, one fleet tanker (T-AOT) and one container ship are maintained to support the three squadrons.

Submarines

Attack submarines (SSN) provide a unique combination of stealth, persistence, and firepower that complements other naval forces. Attack submarines possess potent surface warfare capabilities and are the preferred, most capable weapons systems to execute undersea warfare. Additionally, SSNs provide unique intelligence, surveillance, and reconnaissance (ISR) and strike warfare capabilities that are applicable across the range of military operations (ROMO). SSNs may deploy with CSGs to provide transit or operating area defense, but they are more likely to conduct independent deployments in support of combatant commander or national tasking.

Guided missile submarines (SSGNs) provide stealthy strike capabilities for power projection and conventional deterrence operations. Capable of covert land attack and insertion of special operations forces, SSGNs are independently deployed to accomplish specific tasking by the combatant commanders.

Submarine ISR, sea control and power projection missions are fulfilled both by SSNs and SSGNs. As the SSGNs begin reaching the end of their service lives, starting around 2026, the Navy plans to transition their covert land attack capabilities to other platforms.

Ballistic Missile Submarines (SSBNs)
SSBNs are strategic national assets that provide continuous, uninterrupted and survivable sea-based nuclear deterrence. The SSBN force structure is tied to complex international negotiations and other considerations.

Large Surface Combatants
Inherently versatile with multi-mission platforms, large surface combatants—cruisers and destroyers—support every core capability in the Maritime Strategy. Large surface combatants have two primary power projection tasks: strike, using land attack cruise missiles; and naval surface fires using gun systems in support of forces ashore. While large surface combatants can project power ashore in this direct manner, they also perform sea control tasks that enable other forms of power projection. Aegis cruisers and destroyers conduct IAMD, including maritime ballistic missile defense (BMD); strike warfare; undersea warfare; and surface warfare missions to defend other naval maneuver forces, sustainment forces, and any aggregation of ships that form a sea base.

Large surface combatants support TSC, maritime security and deterrence primarily through episodic engagement with allies and partners that includes maritime interdiction, IAMD, amphibious assault, undersea warfare and surface warfare events. Such multinational training, combined with ongoing operations, enhances interoperability and proficiency, and serves to deter potential adversaries. Large surface combatants are also employed to defend global fleet station (GFS) and other engagement forces when they are employed in uncertain operating environments; merchant shipping in areas plagued by piracy; and to provide HA/DR.

Increasingly, large surface combatants are tasked to provide maritime BMD. BMD operations can be oriented to defend U.S. or partner assets ashore, or to defend units at sea. While every effort is made to concurrently task the multi-mission capabilities of BMD-equipped Aegis cruisers and destroyers, regional BMD missions frequently require stationing the ships in locations where they otherwise would not be employed. This generates the requirement for additional ships beyond the number of large surface combatants necessary for sea control, power projection, and maritime security operations alone.

Supporting these requirements calls for a significant inventory of large surface combatants (both cruisers and destroyers) with a growing number of them configured with BMD capability. BMD ships provide an additional dimension to conventional deterrence that is increasingly significant as ballistic missiles proliferate and become more sophisticated. The demand for BMD is growing rapidly, making it likely that the requirement for BMD-configured large surface combatants will increase over time.

Small Surface Combatants

Small surface combatants are designed to economically counter surface and subsurface anti-access threats in the littoral. Today, frigates and specialized single-mission mine countermeasure (MCM) ships provide these capabilities, but their mission systems and numbers are limited.

The littoral combatant ship (LCS) will address the most pressing capability and capacity shortfalls in the littoral. The LCS sea frame hosts modular mission packages that configure it to conduct mine countermeasures, surface warfare or undersea warfare missions. LCS sea frames with mine countermeasure modules will replace the current inventory of MCMs. The surface warfare module will complement and expand existing fleet capabilities to neutralize small boat threats in the littoral. The undersea warfare module will augment existing fleet capacity to counter the expanding threat posed by quiet diesel submarines. Importantly, the versatility and lift capacity of the LCS sea frame could support a wide range of secondary missions, including Marine and special operations forces afloat staging base support and sea-based fire support.

LCSs are ideally suited for TSC operations, conducted independently or as part of a GFS. By operating in conjunction with joint high speed vessels (JHSVs), riverine craft and expeditionary security boats, LCS can expand Naval Service capacity for security force assistance (SFA) missions that today are conducted predominantly by patrol craft.

The fast, shallow-draft and lift characteristics of the LCS sea frame guarantee that it will support a wide range of future missions and modules that will adaptively address the emerging sea control, maritime security, HA/DR, and sea-based requirements in the littorals.

Major Cutters

Major cutters are versatile, ocean-going vessels built to perform the full range of Coast Guard missions. These include high- and medium-endurance cutters (WHEC and WMEC, respectively). As multi-mission surface combatants, cutters can be deployed overseas to provide forward presence and conduct maritime security tasks. WHECs have the speed and endurance to deploy as part of a strike group to conduct sea control and power projection. WMECs normally deploy independently to support geographic combatant commanders' (GCC) theater campaign plans, humanitarian assistance and disaster response, and are well suited to support GFS tasks. The national security cutter (NSC) and the offshore patrol cutter (OPC) will replace the WHEC and WMEC, respectively.[29]

Patrol Craft

Patrol craft are designed for domestic littoral missions as well as overseas coastal interdiction operations. Overseas, these small combatant craft conduct both maritime security and coastal sea control missions. In the past the Navy and Coast Guard have transferred craft between Services to meet transitory requirements. While successful in the short term, this approach is not effective in a security environment that demands significant domestic and overseas patrol craft capacity. To overcome this challenge, the Naval Service will continue to pursue development of common patrol craft systems to reduce procurement costs and ensure interoperability. The Coast Guard is also in the process of replacing a portion of its patrol boat (PB) fleet with the fast response cutter (FRC).

The Coast Guard inventory must maintain sufficient capacity to support geographic combatant commander TSC plans, expeditionary requirements requested through the Global Force Management process; and overseas contingency operations; in addition to its full suite of statutory domestic missions.

Combat Logistics Force Ships

Combat logistics forces supply underway naval forces with fuel, food, parts, and ammunition. This unique capability enables U.S. naval forces to deploy and remain at sea indefinitely anywhere in the world. The combat logistics force is a key component of U.S. ability to use the sea as maneuver space and to sustain enduring forward presence with very limited overseas access. This element of the support fleet is continuously deployed and manned by rotating civilian mariner crews who carry out these highly specialized non-combat missions—permitting a high proportion of the overall force to be consistently deployed around the world. The capacity to support *globally distributed, mission-tailored forces* as well as *regionally concentrated, credible combat power* calls for a combat logistics force of fast combat support ships (T-AOE), T-AKEs, and underway replenishment oilers (T-AO).

Joint High Speed Vessels

Joint high speed vessels (JHSVs) are designed to quickly move people and materiel within or between regions, significantly enhancing forward logistics support. JHSVs can also fill a wide variety of TSC missions, in addition to supporting maritime security, HA/DR and power projection missions. These multipurpose ships are particularly well suited for GFS and SFA tasks due to their shallow draft, diverse embarkation options, and ability to access small and austere ports. A detailed concept of operations (CONOPS) is under development that will assist the Navy in determining the total requirement for these flexible vessels.

Command and Support Ships

There are a number of ships that support and sustain the continuous forward operations of U.S. naval forces. Command ships (LCC) provide sea-based C2 capability for naval commanders. Submarine tenders (AS) furnish maintenance and logistic support for nuclear attack submarines. Ocean-going tugs (T-ATF) provide the U.S. Navy with towing service and assist in the recovery of downed aircraft and disabled ships. Rescue and salvage ships (T-ARS) render assistance to disabled ships and provide towing, salvage, diving, firefighting and heavy lift capabilities to the fleet. Ocean surveillance ships (T-AGOS) gather global underwater acoustical data to support anti-submarine warfare system development and undersea warfare effectiveness. Dry cargo/ammunition ships (T-AKE) and float-on/float-off mobile landing platforms (MLP) enhance the capacity and flexibility of the three MPS Squadrons. Hospital ships (T-AH) are designed to provide emergency medical care in support of overseas combat operations. In recent years they have had an increasingly profound impact on HA/DR operations, and the Navy will continue to deploy a T-AH from each coast to conduct proactive humanitarian assistance and TSC missions.

Icebreakers

Icebreakers (WAGB) and "ice-capable ships" assure access and assert U.S. policy in the Polar Regions. Emerging and expanding missions in the Arctic and Antarctic Polar Regions highlight the importance of these vessels in the context of the National Fleet policy. Polar icebreakers support science and research; supply remote stations; enforce sovereignty in U.S. waters; conduct Search and Rescue (SAR), marine environmental protection, and maritime law enforcement missions; and establish presence in international waters. They are the only means of providing assured surface access in support of Arctic maritime security and sea control missions. Icebreakers are specifically designed for open-water ice-breaking with reinforced hulls, tailored hull forms, and rapid ballasting systems. Ice-capable ships have strengthened hulls to enable operations in ice-covered and ice-diminished waters, but have limited icebreaking capability. Increased international activity, new transoceanic shipping routes and competition for resources in the Polar Regions will require icebreakers for the foreseeable future. Current operations, maintenance support funding, and employment of these icebreakers involves complex interagency and scientific research community coordination.[30]

Summary: Relating Naval Forces to the Maritime Strategy

The relationship between major Naval Service platforms and the Maritime Strategy's core capabilities—forward presence, maritime security, HA/DR, sea control, power projection and deterrence—are depicted in Table 1 on page 92.

Table 1: Naval Forces Alignment with the Maritime Strategy

Naval Forces \ Core Capabilities	Forward Presence	Maritime Security	HA/DR	Sea Control	Power Projection	Deterrence
Aircraft Carriers	X		X	X	X	X
Aircraft	X	X	X	X	X	X
Amphibious Ships	X	X	X	X	X	X
SSNs	X	X		X	X	X
SSGNs	X	X			X	X
SSBNs					X	X
Large Surface Combatants	X	X		X	X	X
Small Surface Combatants	X	X		X		
Major Cutters	X	X	X	X		X
Patrol Craft	X	X	X	X		X
Combat Logistics Force	X	X	X	X	X	
Hospital Ships	X		X			
Maritime Prepositioning	X		X		X	
JHSV	X	X	X			
Command and Support	X					
Icebreakers[31]	X	X	X	X		X

Summary

NOC 10 describes who we are as a Naval Service, what we believe, where we operate, and what we provide the Nation. In this era of strategic uncertainty, *regionally concentrated* and *globally distributed* naval forces are uniquely capable of preventing conflict and, when necessary, prevailing in war. The ability to overcome diplomatic, geographic, and military impediments to access is critical to projecting power overseas in support of U.S national interests and those of its allies and partners. Naval forces use the sea as maneuver space to overcome these impediments and to respond effectively to a broad range of nuclear, conventional and irregular challenges. To this end, the core capabilities in the Maritime Strategy—forward presence, maritime security, HA/DR, sea control, power projection and deterrence—manifest in the Naval Service, serving to promote peace and prosperity for the common good of the global community.

The Naval Service operates in a security environment characterized by an increasing number of concurrent, diverse challenges, perpetrated by both state and non-state actors, that is evolving toward a new multi-polar balance of global power. The Naval Service recognizes the importance of allies and partners in this environment, and is committed to collaboratively building the interoperability and capacity necessary to share the burden of achieving global maritime security and providing for the common defense of like-minded nations.

The Naval Service capabilities presented in NOC 10 represent a balance carefully designed to address the requirement to concurrently enhance global maritime security, prevent and respond to crises, and defeat very capable adversaries in accordance with the concept. The ideas in NOC 10 will be refined over time through wargaming, experimentation, operational analysis and practical experience—ultimately resulting in changes to the way naval forces are employed. That said, it is unlikely such refinements will diminish the requirement for naval forces in the foreseeable future.

Most importantly, NOC 10 underscores that Sailors, Marines and Coast Guardsmen are, and will always be, the foundation of the Naval Service. They possess the willpower, creativity, inspiration, reason, knowledge, and experience to overcome adversity and accomplish any task. They are the driving force behind successful implementation of the Maritime Strategy.

Annex **A**

The *National Security Strategy, National Defense Strategy, National Military Strategy*, and the *National Strategy for Maritime Security* establish U.S. strategic objectives. The *Unified Command Plan, Guidance for Employment of the Force, Global Force Management Guidance*, and *Joint Strategic Capabilities Plan* provide strategic guidance for joint force organization, deployment, and employment. The *Guidance for Development of the Force* and *Quadrennial Defense Review* provide similar top-level direction for evolving the requisite military capabilities for the future.

Informed by these strategic objectives and guidance, as well as an estimate of trends that will dominate the future security environment, the family of Joint Operations Concepts (JOpsC)[32] describes how operations may be conducted 8 to 20 years in the future in order to provide the conceptual basis for experimentation and capabilities-based assessments.[33] The outcomes of experimentation and assessments underpin investment decisions leading to the development of new military capabilities beyond the Future Years Defense Program (FYDP), ultimately leading to changes in policy and doctrine, organization, training, materiel, leadership and education, personnel, and facilities (DOTMLPF).

The *Joint Operations Concepts Development Process* is defined by Chairman, Joint Chiefs of Staff Instruction 3010.02B, which states that, "Services, combatant commands, and Defense agencies conduct basic research, explore emerging technologies, generate innovative concepts, and conduct experimentation to develop service-unique or joint capabilities. These efforts provide the context for analyzing capabilities for the future joint force. The results of this analysis will influence planning, programming, budgeting and execution (PPBE) decisions as well as identify potential future concepts for the JOpsC family."[34]

The role of Service-generated concepts is further elaborated in Chairman, Joint Chiefs of Staff Instruction 3170.01G, *Joint Capabilities Integration and Development System*, which states that "The Services are responsible for developing Service-specific operational concepts and experimenting within core competencies, supporting joint concept development with Service experimentation, providing feedback from the field, supporting joint experimentation, joint testing and evaluation, and overseeing integration of validated joint DCRs" (DOTMLPF change recommendations).[35]

NOC 10 provides the overarching concept that informs naval participation in joint concept development and experimentation. The material contained in *NOC 10* is to be used in two mutually informative ways. First, it will guide how the Naval Service organizes, deploys, and employs current and programmed capabilities to accomplish near-term (inside the FYDP) implementation of *A Cooperative Strategy for 21ˢᵗ Century Seapower* (CS-21). Second, it will guide our participation in the JOpsC development process, experimentation, and assessment to support long-term (beyond the FYDP) joint capability development. Both of these applications will require development of supporting concepts of operation (CONOPS), whereby approved concepts are applied against likely scenarios in order to inform both near-term and long-term DOTMLPF changes.

Annex **B**

Glossary

advance base—(DOD) A base located in or near an operational area whose primary mission is to support military operations.

amphibious force—(DOD) An amphibious task force and a landing force together with other forces that are trained, organized, and equipped for amphibious operations. Also called AF.

amphibious task force—(DOD) A Navy task organization formed to conduct amphibious operations. The amphibious task force, together with the landing force and other forces, constitutes the amphibious force. Also called ATF.

assault echelon—(DOD) In amphibious operations, the element of a force comprised of tailored units and aircraft assigned to conduct the initial assault on the operational area. Also called AE.

assault follow-on echelon—(DOD) In amphibious operations, that echelon of the assault troops, vehicles, aircraft, equipment, and supplies that, though not needed to initiate the assault, is required to support and sustain the assault. In order to accomplish its purpose, it is normally required in the objective area no later than five days after commencement of the assault landing. Also called AFOE.

civil affairs—(DOD) Designated Active and Reserve component forces and units organized, trained, and equipped specifically to conduct civil affairs activities and to support civil-military operations. Also called CA.

cooperative security locations—(DOD) A facility located outside the United States and U.S. territories with little or no permanent U.S. presence, maintained with periodic Service, contractor, or host-nation support. Cooperative security locations provide contingency access, logistic support, and rotational use by operating forces and are a focal point for security cooperation activities. Also call CSL.

counterinsurgency—(DOD) Those military, paramilitary, political, economic, psychological, and civic actions taken by a government to defeat insurgency. Also called COIN.

cyberspace—(DOD) A global domain within the information environment consisting of the interdependent network of information technology infrastructures, including the Internet, telecommunications networks, computer systems, and imbedded processors and controllers. (Promulgated by the Deputy Secretary of Defense 12 May 2008; inclusion in DOD Dictionary pending.)

defense support of civil authorities—(DOD) Civil support provided under the auspices of the National Response Plan. Also called DSCA.

developmental assistance—(DOD) U.S. Agency for International Development function chartered under chapter one of the Foreign Assistance Act of 1961, primarily designed to promote economic growth and the equitable distribution of its benefits.

DOTMLPF—(DOD) Doctrine, organization, training, materiel, leadership and education, personnel, and facilities.

forcible entry—(DOD) Seizing and holding of a military lodgment in the face of armed opposition.

foreign assistance—(DOD) Assistance to foreign nations, ranging from the sale of military equipment; to donations of food and medical supplies to aid survivors of natural and man-made disasters. U.S. assistance takes three forms—development assistance, humanitarian assistance, and security assistance.

foreign disaster relief—(DOD) Prompt aid that can be used to alleviate the suffering of foreign disaster victims. Normally it includes humanitarian services and transportation; the provision of food, clothing, medicine, beds, and bedding; temporary shelter and housing; the furnishing of medical materiel and medical and technical personnel; and making repairs to essential services.

foreign humanitarian assistance—(DOD) Programs conducted to relieve or reduce the results of natural or man-made disasters or other endemic conditions such as human pain, disease, hunger, or privation that might present a serious threat to life or that can result in great damage to or loss of property. Foreign humanitarian assistance provided by U.S. forces is limited in scope and duration. The foreign assistance provided is designed to supplement or complement the efforts of the host nation civil authorities or agencies that may have the primary responsibility for providing foreign humanitarian assistance. Foreign humanitarian assistance operations are those conducted outside the United States, its territories, and possessions. Also called FHA.

forward operating sites—(DOD) A scalable location outside the United States and U.S. territories intended for rotational use by operating forces. Such expandable "warm facilities" may be maintained with a limited U.S. military support presence and possibly prepositioned equipment. Forward operating sites support rotational rather than permanently stationed forces and are a focus for bilateral and regional training. Also called FOS.

forward presence—(NDP 1) Maintaining forward deployed or stationed forces overseas to demonstrate national resolve, strengthen alliances, dissuade potential adversaries, and enhance the ability to respond quickly to contingency operations.

global fleet station—(GFS CONOPS) A highly visible, positively engaged, persistent sea base of operations from which to interact with partner nation military and civilian populations and the global maritime community. Also called GFS.

global maritime partnerships—(Proposed) An approach to cooperation among maritime nations with a shared stake in international commerce, safety, security, and freedom of the seas. Serves as a basis for building a global consensus on policy principles and for under-taking common activities to address maritime challenges by improving collective capabilities. Also called GMP.

homeland defense—(DOD) The protection of United States sovereignty, territory, domestic population, and critical infrastructure against external threats and aggression or other threats as directed by the President. Also called HD.

humanitarian and civic assistance—(DOD) Assistance to the local populace provided by predominantly U.S. forces in conjunction with military operations and exercises. This assistance is specifically authorized by Title 10, United States Code, Section 401, and funded under separate authorities. Assistance provided under these provisions is limited to (1) medical, dental, veterinary, and preventive medicine care provided in rural areas of a country; (2) construction of rudimentary surface transportation systems; (3) well drilling and construction of basic sanitation facilities; and (4) rudimentary construction and repair of public facilities. Assistance must fulfill unit-training requirements that incidentally create humanitarian benefit to the local populace.

information environment—(DOD) The aggregate of individuals, organizations, and systems that collect, process, disseminate, or act on information.

information operations—(DOD) The integrated employment of the core capabilities of electronic warfare, computer network operations, psychological operations, military deception, and operations security, in concert with specified supporting and related capabilities, to influence, disrupt, corrupt or usurp adversarial human and automated decision making while protecting our own. Also called IO.

insurgency—(DOD) An organized movement aimed at the overthrow of a constituted government through use of subversion and armed conflict.

integration—(DOD) The arrangement of military forces and their actions to create a force that operates by engaging as a whole.

interoperability—1. (DOD, NATO) The ability to operate in synergy in the execution of assigned tasks. 2. (DOD only) The condition achieved among communications-electronics systems or items of communications-electronics equipment when information or services can be exchanged directly and satisfactorily between them and/or their users. The degree of interoperability should be defined when referring to specific cases.

irregular warfare—(DOD) A violent struggle among state and non-state actors for legitimacy and influence over the relevant population(s). Irregular warfare favors indirect and asymmetric approaches, though it may employ the full range of military and other capacities, in order to erode an adversary's power, influence, and will. Also called IW.

landing force—(DOD) A Marine Corps or Army task organization formed to conduct amphibious operations. The landing force, together with the amphibious task force and other forces, constitute the amphibious force. Also called LF.

lighterage—(DOD) The process in which small craft are used to transport cargo or personnel from ship to shore. Lighterage may be performed using amphibians, landing craft, discharge lighters, causeways, and barges.

lodgment—(DOD) A designated area in a hostile or potentially hostile territory that, when seized and held, makes the continuous landing of troops and materiel possible, and provides maneuver space for subsequent operations.

main operating base—(DOD) A facility outside the United States and U.S. territories with permanently stationed operating forces and robust infrastructure. Main operating bases are characterized by command and control (C2) structures, enduring family support facilities, and strengthened force protection measures. Also called MOB.

maritime domain—(DOD) The oceans, seas, bays, estuaries, islands, coastal areas, and the airspace above these, including the littorals.

maritime security operations—(Proposed) Those operations conducted to protect sovereignty and resources, ensure free and open commerce, and to counter maritime-related terrorism, transnational crime, piracy, environmental destruction, and illegal seaborne immigration.

maritime superiority—(DOD). That degree of dominance of one force over another that permits the conduct of maritime operations by the former and its related land, maritime, and air forces at a given time and place without prohibitive interference by the opposing force.

military engagement—(DOD) Routine contact and interaction between individuals or elements of the Armed Forces of the United States and those of another nation's armed forces, or foreign and domestic civilian authorities or agencies to build trust and confidence, share information, coordinate mutual activities, and maintain influence.

Naval Logistics Integration—(DON) A coordinated Navy-Marine Corps effort to establish an integrated naval logistics capability that can operate seamlessly whether afloat or ashore.

noncombatant evacuation operations—(DOD) Operations directed by the Department of State or other appropriate authority, in conjunction with the Department of Defense, whereby noncombatants are evacuated from foreign countries when their lives are endangered by war, civil unrest, or natural disaster to safe havens or to the United States. Also called NEOs.

power projection—(DOD) The ability of a nation to apply all or some of its elements of national power—political, economic, informational, or military—to rapidly and effectively deploy and sustain forces in and from multiple dispersed locations to respond to crises, to contribute to deterrence, and to enhance regional stability.

seabasing—(DOD) The deployment, assembly, command, projection, reconstitution, and re-employment of joint power from the sea without reliance on land bases within the operational area.

sea control operations—(DOD) The employment of naval forces, supported by land and air forces as appropriate, in order to achieve military objectives in vital sea areas. Such operations include destruction of enemy naval forces, suppression of enemy sea commerce, protection of vital sea lanes, and establishment of military superiority in areas of naval operations.

security assistance—(DOD) Group of programs authorized by the Foreign Assistance Act of 1961, as amended, and the Arms Export Control Act of 1976, as amended, or other related statutes by which the United States provides defense articles, military training, and other defense-related services by grant, loan, credit, or cash sales in furtherance of national policies and objectives. Also called SA.

security cooperation—(DOD) All Department of Defense interactions with foreign defense establishments to build defense relationships that promote specific U.S. security interests, develop allied and friendly military capabilities for self-defense and multinational operations, and provide U.S. forces with peacetime and contingency access to a host nation.

space—(DOD) A medium like the land, sea, and air within which military activities shall be conducted to achieve U.S. national security objectives.

stability operations—1. (DOD) An overarching term encompassing various military missions, tasks, and activities conducted outside the United States in coordination with other instruments of national power to maintain or reestablish a safe and secure environment, provide essential governmental services, emergency infrastructure reconstruction, and humanitarian relief. 2. (DoDD 3000.05) Military and civilian activities conducted across the spectrum from peace to conflict to establish or maintain order in States and regions.

strike—(DOD) An attack to damage or destroy an objective or a capability.

terrorism—(DOD) The calculated use of violence or the threat of violence to inculcate fear; intended to coerce or to intimidate governments or societies in the pursuit of goals that are generally political, religious, or ideological.

Endnotes

1   Per Title 10, U.S. Code, section 101, and Title 14 U.S.C. §1-3, the Coast Guard is "a military service and a branch of the armed forces of the United States at all times." The Coast Guard may at any time provide forces and/or perform its military functions in support of naval component or combatant commanders. Also, "Upon the declaration of war if congress so directs in the declaration or when the President directs," the entire Coast Guard may operate as a specialized service in the Department of the Navy. The Coast Guard is also, at all times, a Federal maritime law enforcement agency. Pursuant to 14 U.S.C. § 89(a), the Coast Guard has broad powers to "make inquiries, examinations, inspections, searches, seizures, and arrests upon the high seas and waters over which the United States has jurisdiction, for the prevention, detection, and suppression of violations of the laws of the United States."

2   These terms were originated by Harvard professor Joseph Nye in a number of books and articles. Nye's concept of "soft power" espouses that a nation's culture (where it is attractive to others), political values (when lived up to), and foreign policy (when seen as legitimate and having moral authority) may "attract" a population away from competing ideologies, providing a complement to "hard power" such as military force. For example, during the Cold War the West used "hard power" to deter Soviet aggression and "soft power" to erode faith in Communism.

3   NDS 08, p. 2.

4   "Range of military operations (ROMO)" is a term that encompasses the myriad activities in which naval forces participate. These vary from deterring or winning wars through conventional, unconventional, or nuclear means to the various activities conducted in partnership with a diverse array of joint, interagency, multinational or non-governmental organizations which promote safety and security as well as ease human suffering.

5   "Surge" is diverting forces from other operational, training, or maintenance activities to provide the capability or capacity necessary to satisfy a higher priority event.

6   Hughes, Wayne, "Implementing the Seapower Strategy," Naval War College Review, (Newport, RI: Spring 2008), pp. 57-58.

7   Huntington, Samuel P., "National Policy and the Transoceanic Navy," U.S. Naval Institute Proceedings, (Annapolis, MD: May, 1954), p. 491.

8   Mullen, Admiral Michael G., USN, Capstone Concept for Joint Operations, (Washington, D.C.: Department of Defense, 15 January 2008), p. 3.

9   Although not an approved doctrinal term, "connectors" is commonly used within joint concept development and experimentation to describe those air and naval surface craft used to shuttle personnel and resources between bases, afloat platforms, and locations ashore.

10   Maritime prepositioning ships carry Marine Corps equipment, supplies and ammunition as well as Seabee construction equipment, expeditionary airfields, and field hospital cargo, providing utility for a range of operations. Operated by the Military Sealift Command (MSC), they are forward postured where they can quickly close on areas of vital national interest. Like other MSC ships, they have a "T" before their type-codes. To further distinguish them from combatants, their names are prefaced by "USNS" (United States Naval Ship) versus "USS" (United States Ship).

11   Turner, Stansfield, "Missions of the Navy," (Newport, RI: U.S. Naval Strategy in the 1970's, Naval War College Newport Papers, No. 30, September 2007), p. 49.

12   Data provided by U.S. Fleet Forces Command as of 23 September 2009 and is based on a comparison of force requests for fiscal years 2007 through 2011.

13   USN considers all service members assigned to support Joint Manning Documents (JMD), Ad-Hoc, In-Lieu-Of (ILO) and Service Augment requirements as Individual Augmentees.

14   The Coast Guard currently provides LEDET coverage of 2.0 for CENTCOM and 5.5 for SOUTHCOM, respectively. Increases in funding and end strength are needed to support growing combatant command (COCOM) demand as follows: 2.0 each to AFRICOM, CENTCOM, EUCOM, PACOM (8.0) and 5.5 to SOUTHCOM. The future requirement for LEDETs is a 13.5 presence.

15   Current demand is a 1.0 PSU presence in the CENTCOM AOR and 1.0 PSU presence for SOUTHCOM.

16   For further discussion of EMIO, see Joint Publication 3-03, *Joint Interdiction*.

17   Elleman, Bruce A., *Waves of Hope*, (Newport, RI: Naval War College Newport Papers, Volume 28, February 2007), p.117.

18   Cobble, W. Eugene, Gaffney, H. H., and Gorenburg, Dmitry, *For the Record: All U.S. Forces' Responses to Situations, 1970-2000*, (Alexandria, VA: Center for Naval Analyses, May 2005), p. 8.

19   Heinl, Robert D., Jr., *Soldiers of the Sea*, (Annapolis, MD: U.S. Naval Institute, 1962), p. 604.

20   Churchill, Winston S., *The Second World War: Their Finest Hour*, (Boston, MA: Houghton Mifflin Company, 1949), p. 479.

21   Liddell Hart, B. H., *Deterrence or Defense*, (New York: Frederick A. Praeger, Inc., 1960), p. 128.

22   Mullen, Admiral, Michael G., U.S. Navy, *Capstone Concept for Joint Operations*, (Washington, D.C.: Department of Defense, 15 January 2008), p. 6.

23   The data cited in this paragraph has been obtained from multiple sources, to include: the electronic *Chronologies of the United States Marine Corps, 1982-2007* and the official histories produced by the History & Museums Division, Headquarters, U.S. Marine Corps; *SEA POWER FOR A NEW ERA: 2006 Program Guide to the U.S. Navy*, Appendix A "Navy-Marine Corps Crisis Response and Combat Actions," produced by the Office of the Chief of Naval Operations; and the *Naval Review Issues* of the U.S. Naval Institute *Proceedings*, 2003-2006.

24   For example, current high-speed intra-theater connectors are capable of offloading onto austere facilities in a secure area. Increased use of expeditionary causeway systems or development of connectors may further exploit that characteristic to reduce reliance on existing infrastructure, as would the development of future connectors capable of offloading near-shore or on the beach.

25   Mahan, Alfred T. *Armaments and Arbitration: or, the Place of Force in the International Relations of States*. (New York: Harper & Brothers, 1912) p. 105.

26   The core capabilities articulated in the Maritime Strategy establish the ways and means that naval forces apply to achieve deterrence, and align with the Deterrence Operations Joint Operating Concept. Through their inherent force projection, active and passive defense, global strike, domain awareness, command and control, and forward presence ways, naval forces possess the means to impose unacceptable costs, deny adversaries the benefits of their aggression, and encourage adversary restraint.

27   Mullen, Michael G., "It's Time for a New Deterrence Model," (Washington, DC: Joint Force Quarterly, Issue 51, 4th Quarter 2008), p. 3.

28   MSC ships have a "T" before the type-code. To further distinguish them from combatants, their names are prefaced by "USNS" (United States Naval Ship) versus "USS" (United States Ship).

29   Combatant commander demand calls for a 2.0 major cutter presence to meet theater campaign plan requirements (to include security cooperation and security force assistance) in Mediterranean/ African littoral waters and the Western Pacific/Indian Ocean. Demand for the Eastern Pacific and Caribbean Basin calls for a 6.0 cutter presence.

30   The current Icebreaker demand requires a 1.0 presence in the Arctic and 1.0 in the Antarctic.

31   Icebreakers support Forward Presence. They also support Maritime Security, HA/DR, Sea Control and Deterrence in ice-covered and ice-diminished waters; Coast Guard icebreakers are the only means of providing assured surface access.

32 The JOpsC family uses The Joint Operational Environment – The World Through 2020 and Beyond, An Evolving Joint Perspective: Joint Warfare and Crisis Resolution in the 21st Century, and Mapping the Global Future: Report of the National Intelligence Council's 2020 Project to provide insights into the dominant trends shaping the future security environment over the next 20 years.

33 All concepts in the JOpsC family are posted at: http://www.dtic.mil/futurejointwarfare.

34 CJCSI 3010.02B may be viewed at: http://www.dtic.mil/futurejointwarfare/concepts/cjcsi3010_02b.pdf.

35 CJCSI 3170.01G may be viewed at: http://www.dtic.mil/cjcs_directives/cdata/unlimit/3170_01.pdf.